AF657645

AF657645

Dynamics of Ethnicity
A Study of Select Contemporary American Novelists

Dynamics of Ethnicity
A Study of Select Contemporary American Novelists

Dr. Rabi Narayan Samantaray

ADHYAYAN

ADHYAYAN PUBLISHERS & DISTRIBUTORS
New Delhi-110002

Published by
ADHYAYAN PUBLISHERS & DISTRIBUTORS
4378/4B, 105, J.M.D. House, Murari Lal Street
Ansari Road Darya Ganj, New Delhi - 110002
Ph.: 011-23263018, 011-23277156, Fax: 23280028
Email: adhyayanpublishers@yahoo.com

Dynamics of Ethnicity A Study of Select Contemporary American Novelists

© Author
Edition 2011
ISBN 978-81-8435-267-2

The responsibility for facts stated, opinion expressed or conclusions reached and plagiarism, if any, in this book is entirely that of the author/ editor. The publisher bears no responsibility for them whatsoever.

Printed in India

Published by Harish Chandra Yadav for Adhyayan Publishers & Distributors, Delhi. Laser Typesetting at Jain Computers and Printed at Tarun Offset Printers, Delhi

Dedicated to those
for whom, pursuit of
knowledge is an obsession.

Preface

Dynamics of Ethnicity: A Study of select contemporary American novelists is a work on the various facets of American ethnic literature in the light of the selected novels by Bernard Malamud, Richard Wright, and Leslie Marmon Silko. The society in the United States of America is traditionally believed to be a "melting pot" where people from various nationalities come to live together by losing their individual national identities. But in modern times, several American social phenomena reveal that the melting pot theory has become a myth as the modern American society does not stand for what the implications of "melting pot" suggest. Various ethnic communities in the United States have developed the tendency to retain their ethnic identities as it has become a source of strength for them. The American society is peopled by several ethnic communities.

The scope of my book has been restricted to three ethnic communities, namely, Jewish-American, Afro-American, and Native-American as represented by Bernard Malamud, Richard Wright, and Leslie Marmon Silko respectively. The pictures of American ethnicity that we get in the novels of these three writers are different from one another. In Malamud's work, the immigrant experience is more peripheral and more central than in writers of comparable background. Malamud is considered to be a Jewish-American writer because he writes about the Jews and some elements of the Jewish milieu. It may be constructive to probe a bit in order to see what kind of Jewish world that Malamud has presented in his novels.

Richard Wright's novels exhibit another dimension of American ethnic literature. He is very much vocal and does not hesitate to articulate the racial feelings of the Afro-Americans. His characters try to assert their place in the American society. The Afro-Americans demand equal amount of rights and opportunities as their white counterparts enjoy in the society. The fictional characters of Wright are rebels, as they question the basic values of the American society. His characters also follow the path of violence and they oppose the validity of several social institutions.

Native-American literature derives its strength from the richness of American heritage. It also shows the process of cultural transformation and innovation that sustains the creative survival rather than the more familiar narratives of psychological and social disintegration of Native-American cultures in the face of western colonization. Leslie Marmon Silko is of mixed cultural and racial origin. She is part Laguna, part Mexican and part white. Silko makes an effort to create a hybrid literary form in which the Pueblo oral traditions and western literary forms and narratives are juxtaposed and intercut as part of a complex process of mutual transformation. Silko is committed to literary and cultural innovation. She deploys and changes various Pueblo and western narratives throughout her novels, particularly the way in which she either uses traditional oral stories in the new contexts or changes these stories to meet the new contexts and the way in which these traditional stories are altered and mediated by being brought into alignment with western literary forms. Silko's writings present a case of conflict between the two sets of values.

The "introduction" to the book aims at offering an insight into the spectrum of ethnic literature in the American context. This part of the book discusses the role and relevance of the Jewish-American, Afro-American, and Native-American literatures in the context of the American ethnic scenario. The second chapter would concentrate on Bernard Malamud, an exponent of Jewish-American literature. I have taken up three selected novels by Bernard Malamud, namely, *The Assistant, The Fixer* and *The Tenants.* All these three novels are based upon ethnic issues and are directly relevant to my book. While the locale of *The Assistant* and *The Tenants* is the United States, the locale of *The Fixer* is Tsarist Russia. In fact, Russia is used as a metaphor for the United States of America. In all these three novels, the problems of the Jews living in an alien land are highlighted. The third chapter would discuss the literary contribution of Richard Wright with reference to his selected novels. His *Native Son* is a significant work of art dealing with the theme of black ethnicity. This novel brought about a revolutionary change in the thought process of the Afro-Americans and it made them aware of their predicament in the American Society. His *Black Boy* is an autobiographical novel based on the theme of racism and hence finds an analysis in this chapter. The fourth chapter deals with Leslie Marmon Silko, the first woman Native-American novelist. I have deliberately chosen Silko because her literary works record the value system of the Native-

American race. Though Silko's literary output is very rich, I have taken up two of her novels which are vibrant with the ideas of ethnicity. They are: *Ceremony* and *Almanac of the Dead.* Both the novels record typical Native American values. These novels also offer a very meaningful insight into the cultural heritage of the Native-Americans from a literary perspective. The "Conclusion" substantiates the major themes of all the three chapters and moves towards the findings of the book. It shows how the tone of ethnicity prevails in the writings of all the three writers and the manner in which they conform to a definite ethnic tradition.

October 22, 2010. **Rabi Narayana Samantaray**

Contents

1

Introduction

The term "ethnicity" in the American context refers to the descendants of the European immigrants in the United States of America. However, "ethnicity" in the wider sense refers to any differentiation based on nationality, race and religion. A significant part of the problem in evaluating the meaning of ethnicity in the American context lies in the fact that some groups that Americans think of as "ethnic" are constituted by religion as in the case of Jews; some by nationality as in the case of Poles; some by religion and nationality as in the case of Irish Catholics; yet some by race, as in the case of the Blacks and some by region as in the case of the Native-Americans. This has given rise to a number of interpretations and definitions of the term "ethnicity". Different writers have defined the term differently. In the words of Joe R.Feagin, "ethnicity" refers to "a group which is socially distinguished or set apart, by others and/or by itself , primarily on the basis of cultural or nationality characteristics"(9).However, the definition of ethnicity as given by Schemerhorn seems more appropriate to my purpose. It runs as follows: "A collectivity within a larger society having real or putative common ancestry, memories of a shared historical past, and a cultural focus on one or more symbolic elements defined as the epitome of their peoplehood"(123).

It has been observed that two factors have shaped most analyses of the ethnicity phenomenon: the domination factor and the assimilation factor. The domination factor is most frequently used in the study of colonialism. It is basically a picture of conflict in which one group is perceived as controlling and usually oppressing the other group. The assimilation factor is more accommodating in its assumptions and focuses on the adjustment of two cultures to each other after encounter and interspersion. Its concerns are "culture contact", in which the culture of the host society is threatened by the culture of a numerically inferior but politically dominant group, or "acculturation", in which the culture of the immigrant group is threatened by that of a numerically and politically dominant host society. Both factors stand on the way of homogenization in respect to the political and structural pattern of the society.

The picture of the American society, as it appears to us, is an amalgamation of different cultures merging into one common "American" culture. As Fabian remarked, "it is often overlooked that immigrants, when they arrive in a new country, do not constitute a group or a community-they may become one over time" (7). When we use the expressions like "Jewish-American", "Afro-American", and "Native-American", we tend to place a hyphen to establish a link between the ethnic groups and America which is suggestive of a sense of equality and not a way of withdrawing from the rest of the society. In an Urban environment where everyone including the Native American was something else besides being "American", one had to be an ethnic to find one's place on the map. The pertinent question about American ethnicity is not why there is differentiation in American society but why the ethnic coding system becomes a relevant chart of differentiation for many Americans under certain sets of circumstances. Ethnicity reveals itself as a relatively safe form of differentiation. While there may be conflict and competition among the various ethnic groups, the conflict is rarely violent. Society has implicitly legitimized ethnic differentiation and has provided protocols and processes whereby the potential conflict that could arise from such differentiation is minimized. Fabian argues that ethnicization is the "process by which immigrants from one society become ethnic in another" (16). She describes the process as follows: "people, while living in their own society, take their culture and identity to a great extent for granted. When, due to some historical circumstances, they leave, this unproblematic nature of reality disappears. But questions of cultural identity arise only when immigrants are asked by the host society, 'Who are you'?" (17).

We might argue that the most striking aspect of American ethnic differentiation is that, by definition, ethnic boundaries are supposed to be permeable. The ethnic collectivity does indeed provide a rationale for self-definition, and in all self-definitions there is implicit some sort of separation from those who do not have the same self-definition. But even the ethnic self-definition in the United States is more concerned with defining oneself as part of the American Society and not separate from it. Under such circumstances ethnic group boundaries are permeable, because the political and social culture has decreed that they ought to be permeable and because they have been so structured.

The concept of ethnicity is very much predominant in the realm of American literature. But the scope of my book will be restricted to three ethnic communities such as Jewish-American, the Afro-American and the Native-American represented by three novelists, namely, Bernard Malamud, Richard Wright, and Leslie Marmon Silko respectively and my attempt would be to discuss some selected novels of these writers in order to show how they have dealt with the theme of ethnicity in their writings. In fact, the contributions of ethnic writers have added to the complexity and grandeur of modern American literature. Of all the ethnic groups, the blacks and the Jews have been the most prominent groups facing the problems of a pluralist society. Whereas the blacks have been strident in registering their protest against racial discrimination, the Jews have been strenuously moving from the circumference to the center of the American social structure. Haunted by their traumatic past, immigrant Jews from Spain, Portugal, Germany and particularly from Russia have constantly tried to acquire a safe refuge for them from religious persecution. Their major problem has been that of assimilation and of identity. They have been striving hard to acculturate themselves into the mainstream American culture without losing their Jewish value-system and Judaic heritage. For the American-Jewish novelists, their main concern has been with the 'Complex fate' of being a Jew in America. Bernard Malamud, Saul Bellow and Philip Roth, among others, have rendered this experience of acculturation in their writings. While Bellow dislikes being called a Jew,[1] Roth has been a severe critic of Orthodox Judaism. Both of them are aware of their Jewish assumptions, but their emphasis has been on secular trans-ethnic values. Bellow's response to Jewishness, in this context, is quite striking; he regards himself as a 'Midwesterner and not a Jew'. He further goes on to say "I am often described as a Jewish writer in much the same way one might be called a Samoan astronomer or an Eskimo cellist or Zulu Gainsborough expert. There is some oddity about it. I am a Jew, and I have written some books. I have tried to fit my soul into the Jewish-writer category, but it does not feel comfortably accommodated there" (Bellow 72).It suggests that Bellow clearly does not wish to be included in the category of American Jewish novelists, or of novelists of Jewish origin settled in America.

Roth is another Jewish writer who rejects the idea of the Jews being the elect, and indicts the mood of racial superiority and "self-congratulation" among his co-religionists. When the orthodox sections among the Jews accused him of hysterical "Self hate", he defends his position in these words: "The question really is, who is going to address men and women like men and women, and who like children. If there are Jews who have begun to find the stories, the novelists tell more provocative and pertinent than the sermons of some of the rabbis, perhaps it is because there are regions of feeling and consciousness in them which cannot be reached by the oratory of self-congratulation and self-pity" (Roth 169). Compared to these vocal assertions against Jewishness, Malamud's position is qualitatively different. Unlike Bellow and Roth, the stamp of Jewishness is invariably assigned to the creative genius of Malamud who neither condones the Judaic orthodoxy nor does he intemperately flout Jewish moral conventions. He is emphatic in asserting that there is a broad humanistic concern in all his tales about the Jews. He is equally forthright in affirming that he is a Jew and fully conscious of his heritage of Diaspora and suffering. His statement that 'every man is a Jew' tends to suggest that Malamud looks upon the Jew as a paradigm of human values and not a creature of a chosen tribe. Malamud himself explains his point of view when he says that he writes about the Jews because he knows something about them though he is not afraid to go from Jewish experiences to non-Jewish experiences. When he is specifically asked about his Jewish subject matter, his answer is : "As for 'Jewishness', it's there of course, and I draw from its love of morality to strengthen my own, and from its history as symbol of man's struggle, and use whatever other material excites my imagination. I am not a religious Jew" (Ducharme 95).

Another important effective means to approach the American ethnic literature is to look into the contributions of Afro-American writers who deal with the plight of the Afro-Americans who constitute a sizable portion of American population. The Afro-American literature gained prominence only after World War II, perhaps the most exciting and innovative genre practised by historians of the United States. In 1941 the American anthropologist Melville J.Herskovits published *The Myth of the Negro Past* which revolutionized the way educated persons thought of African history. The effect of the earlier notion, that Herskovists demolished, was a dual one: first of all, it had been believed that black Africa, the home land of American Negroes, was a cultural desert that had contributed nothing to the world and therefore, the slaves who came here were "primitive savages without even the vestiges of a viable culture;"

Second, that whatever culture Africans might have had in the old world was totally lost, except, perhaps for some "Savage" survivals in the fields of music and dance.

In due course of time, the emergence of a native born Afro-American majority gave rise to a new kind of ethnic scenario. By the time of the American Revolution most blacks were more American than African, but society used their color to keep them apart and segregated them from as much of American life as it could. Black Americans, like all other immigrant groups, excepting the American Indians, are descended from relatively recent immigrants; they have shared most of the experiences of American life, but those experiences have been modified by their "different" position in the United States Society. No one ever expressed this unique position better than W.E.B. Dubois who wrote early in the twentieth century "One ever feels his two ness-an American, a Negro, two souls, two thoughts, two unreconciled strivings; two warring ideals in one dark body, whose dogged strength alone keeps it from being torn asunder. The history of the American Negro is the history of this strife, this longing to attain self conscious manhood, to merge his double self into a truer and better self"(278).

Persecution, pain, and suffering, then, have been the common ingredients in Jewish-American and Afro-American literature. But, despite these similarities contemporary Afro-American and Jewish-American literature seem quite different from each other. Studies of Jewish fiction generally emphasize its compassionate and humanistic values; in contrast, analyses of black literature center on its rage and violence. In an essay, "Negroes and Jews. An encounter in America", Leslie Fielder notes the transformation of the Negro from "Uncle Tom" into "Bigger Thomas", from the "pitiable nigger" into the "angry warrior" (*No! In Thunder* 236). Unwilling to appease the Whites, contemporary black writers have rejected literary ancestors like William Wells Brown, James Weldon Johnson, and Charles Chesnutt, who "shape their stories to suit a White audience" (Emanuel and Gross 3). In comparison with Jewish works which preach compassion and celebrate life, the tone of much recent black writing is resentful and often inflammatory. Yet, in the hands of Imamu Baraka or John A.Williams, violence has become redemptive, a necessary act of affirmation.

Richard Nathaniel Wright, an American author whose outspoken protest against racial prejudice has made him perhaps the most eloquent spokesperson for his generation of blacks in America. A rising tide of violence characterizes Wright's fiction from *Uncle Tom's Children* to *Native Son* and *The Outsider*. Wright's characters need to express themselves. When Bigger Thomas finally begins to comprehend his life, he gropes for words, trying to communicate his agony to Max, his lawyer. Wright's protagonists, like Malamud's have a need to communicate their suffering, but they are denied relief. Scorned by the Whites and feared by the slavish Negroes, the Afro-Americans are truly outsiders whose only recourse appears to be violence. Even Richard Wright, who learned to use words as a weapon, was capable of brutality. In the autobiographical novel, *Black Boy*, the author, a young boy, rebels against his authoritarian father by killing an innocent kitten. The absence of freedom provokes Wright's rebels to attack their family and friends: sometimes in self-defense and, sometimes in anger and hatred. *Black Boy* serves as a partial model for Wright's other works in which the protagonists reflect their brutal environments. Although Richard Wright never raised his hands to his mother, he defended himself with a kitchen knife and razor blades against his Aunt Addie's and Uncle Tom's attempts to "break spirit" (*Black Boy* 140). In his autobiographical *Black Boy* which came out in the year 1945 Wright reveals in bitter personal terms the devastating impact of racial prejudice on a black person in the United States. As the father of a militant Afro-American literature, Wright provides a contrast with Bernard Malamud, acclaimed as "the most Jewish of American Jewish writers".

The sixties of the twentieth century saw a vibrant phase in American ethnic literature. One of the most active debates of the hyperactive sixties was the one over the use of politics and social concerns as important parameters for determining the worth of fiction. It was a debate especially applicable and frequently applied to black fiction. America's three best-known black writers – Richard Wright, Ralph Ellison and James Baldwin– were all in one way or another implicated in the argument. Wright was praised and damned, posthumously because of his apparent commitment to the use of literature as a political weapon in the war against White Racism. Ellison received the same treatment for holding similar views and Baldwin turned away from his apolitical stance and in order to struggle to maintain prominence or to achieve it in the black revolution, wrote increasingly racially aggressive essays and propagandistic fiction. It may be said of these three writers that they have captured in their fiction those modes that characterize racial life in America in the modern era. In their fiction, we can see the signs of a turning point in the black art and culture and a greater freedom in the way blacks think about themselves and the Whites' attitude towards them. In *Notes of a Native Son,* James Baldwin described his own obsession with "race" in his fiction: "I have not written about being a Negro at such length because I expect that to be my only subject, but only because it was the gate I had to unlock before I could hope to write about anything else" (8). One must learn to be "black" in the American Society, precisely because "blackness" is a socially produced category. Accordingly, many black authors address similar themes and repeat the cultural and linguistic codes of a common symbolic geography. For these reasons, we can think of them as forming a literary tradition of their own.

Richard Wright once argued, polemically, that if white racism did not exist, then black literature would not exist, and he predicted the demise of the latter with the cessation of the former. It is difficult to deny that certain elements of African American culture are the products of cross-cultural encounters with white racism. But, black culture is a self-enclosed mythos, existing apart from the social dynamism of white racism. Development in African American literature has helped to reveal the factitious nature of an "American" identity; that which had been systematically excluded has now been revoiced as a mainstream culture.

Another important ethnic voice that has emerged in the context of the American ethnic literature is that of the Native Americans, whose literature reflects their ethnic consciousness and their sense of "loss". Traditionally called "Indians", Native Americans have suffered from an amazing variety of stereotyped images, from the wooden cigar store figure, to the bloodthirsty savage of the movies, to the noble primitive of some novels as depicted in the writings of Michael Dorris, Louise Erdrich and James Welch. Coupled with this, there has been a tendency to ignore the past and present reality of Native American life. The history of Native-Americans is replete with strange ironies and popular distortions. An important point to note in this context is that the expression, "Indian" was used by European-American settlers. The naming of Native American societies by the Europeans reflects their subordination, because not a single major tribe of theirs has been recorded in most history books under its own name. Native Americans at the time of the European invasion were a diverse collection of societies with peculiar differences in languages, customs, rituals, and beliefs.

The stereotypes that are associated with the Native Americans have developed in the four centuries of their conflict with the Europeans between the early 1500s and the late 1800s which were predominant in rationalizing enslavement and land theft. One early myth, a strange mixture of positive appreciation and patronizing prejudice, was that of the primitive "child of nature" or "noble savage". The European settlers were rudely shocked to see the unwillingness of the indigenous residents to submit to the "civilizing pressures" of the missionaries and the farmers who were seeking land. This fierce Native American resistance gave rise to new stereotypes of "cruel savage" or the "primitive hunter". The "blood thirsty savage" image became prevalent after the first battle with the Native Americans' resistance to the encroachment of their land. By the mid 1600s Europeans in New England and Virginia wrote that the Native Americans were the wild beasts who should be hunted down like other savage animals. Puritan leaders such as Cotton Mather saw them as agents of the devil. Most prominent European

Americans would for the next few centuries, see the Native population as "animals" rather than from the sentimental perspective of earlier philosophers.The Native Americans found themselves as a unique subordinate group in a number of ways. They were the descendants of the only group which did not immigrate to North America in the last six hundred years. They were brought into the European - American sphere in a three hundred year epoch during which they fought bloody, and occasionally successful battles with the invaders. After the long reservation era, a long line of bureaucrats and officials emerged, all seeking to dominate or exploit the Native Americans. Stereotyped as inferior, primitive or savage, a variety of Native American tribes have suffered exploitation and discrimination in the economic, political, religious and educational spheres. In the economic sphere, they have seen their lands taken and relocated in inhospitable cities. Of course, recent decades have seen some positive changes. However, the economic progress has remained very slow. In recent years, "Red Pride" advocates have highlighted the cultural uniqueness of the Native Americans' respect for community and for ecology. Calls for maintaining their cultural distinctiveness and recognizing their superiority have also been heard. In the case of most ethnic minorities in the United States, the immigrants of first generation have found both acculturation and assimilation difficult. It is the second or third generation that finds the acceptance of the dominant society's cultural elements and values less difficult. However, in the case of the American Indian, there is no first, second or third generation. Among the Indians, acculturation comes very slowly to the older people, especially those who are staying on reservations. Away from their culture areas, separated from their brother Indians, and tempted by the exciting new wonders of the white society, the Urban Indian usually casts aside the old culture. It is here that inter personal relationships between Whites and Indians becomes an accepted phenomenon and inter racial marriage is not unusual. Acculturation has come most easily to those Indian groups whose aboriginal socio cultural organization was weak or unstable. When the Whites moved through the Great Basin region into the Pacific coastal areas, they found Indian societies unable to cope with the rapid changes. In the American southwest, however, the Pueblos, Zunis, and Hopis had reached a fairly high level of development and thus had "built-in" barriers to have a unique position in regard to citizenship, since they existed prior to any European government. However, some groups like the Iroquois continue to argue that they are not citizens of the United States and do not want to be her citizens.

The flourishing of Native American literature, like the very survival of Native peoples on the continent has happened against incredible odds. The twentieth century has witnessed the emergence of a very large group of accomplished writers. The flourishing of Indian writings is, in fact, an historic moment to celebrate the talent and diversity of the Native American community. While it is very difficult to generalize about Native American writers, certainly the influence of story telling and the oral tradition is deeply pervasive in Indian literature. The Native American writers very well fit into a storytelling tradition. All of them, in fact, acknowledge the influence of the oral tradition on their works. While they inevitably draw upon traditional songs and stories, the Native American writers are actively re-imagining them within the historical context and the actual experience of contemporary Native American life. Initially the only written texts of American Indian stories and songs came from anthropologists, who would visit tribes to gather stories transcribing them to be published in anthropology and folklore journals. The Native Americans literature is a very powerful institution to falsify the notion of the "vanishing red man". The Native American writers have assumed a greater responsibility of preserving and perpetuating their culture through their writings. Though Native American literature is characterized by elements of diversity, it is even possible to speak of a uniquely Native American literature. According to N.Scott Momaday, American Indian writers do share something in common, although it manifests itself in different ways. Momaday is of the opinion that all the Native American writers have a sense of the heritage and that they have the benefits of an oral literature that goes back on the continent for 30,000 years. Momaday thinks that though all the Native American writers do not follow the same pattern, there is a common denominator. The Native American writers draw on things that have an existence that is indigenous and very strong and it is not the same as other American writers have.

Leslie Marmon Silko, being a Native American novelist, became a meeting ground of cultures, traditions and new ideas. She grew up with a deep love for Laguna Pueblo stories, believing that storytelling is more than an entertainment or a way to pass on values and traditions. For her, Storytelling is a kind of ritual ceremony that links the Native people with their land. Her goal has been to use the gift of story telling to promote the cultural survival of her people. She tries to fuse old and new Laguna Pueblo rituals and ceremonies to meet the present day realities of reservation life by showing how traditional stories apply to and live in the modern world. She fights not just to preserve old stories but also to recognize their essence today and to mould traditional story telling into modern reality. A visionary who presents the interrelatedness of all things, Silko brings to life the courageous and challenging existence of people often overlooked and dismissed. Her writings respect tradition while still promoting the essential change to ensure that the Laguna Pueblo culture survives. Her writings inspire hope and possibility for a people who have received little encouragement from other voices.

In the 1960s and 1970s curiosity about Native Americans increased greatly. Bestselling books such as Vine Deloria's *Custer Died for your sins,* Dee Brown's *Bury my Heart at Wounded Knee,* and Ruth Beebe Hill's *Hanta yo* symbolized the growing interest in the area, as did the increased popularity of such Native American writers as N.Scott Momaday, Alonzo Lopez, and James Welch. For the first time, people were beginning to discard a few of their traditional stereotypes, and they were just beginning to sense the distinctiveness of Native American culture-its holistic independence from the assumptions of western civilization for nearly forty thousand years. Native Americans lived and travelled throughout the continent without significantly altering its environmental heritage or balance; they were at peace with their surroundings. But only four centuries of European civilization seemingly had changed the country forever. The traditional faith in "Manifest Destiny" with its emphasis on expansion, progress, unbridled growth, as well as racial superiority had a new generation of critics in the 1960s and 1970s as modern society began to choke on its own materialism, and as Americans suffered through inflation, unemployment, pollution, and chronic energy shortages, the world of Native Americans suddenly took on a new meaning; to some it even became an appealing alternative to the endless series of crises. Perhaps the Native Americans had been right all along in their approach to life, death and change. Even then, of course, most non-Native Americans had no appreciation for the structure and complexity of Native American values; but they did for the first time, realize that Native Americans were indeed different, that their vision of living and dying was not at all like that of Europeans, and that they were not likely to change easily.

My purpose of incorporating three ethnic writers into the scope of the book is to offer a reasonably fair picture of American ethnic literature. An element of "ethnic awareness" is common to Jewish-American, Afro-American, and Native American literatures. Bernard Malamud, Richard Wright, and Leslie Marmon Silko are all champions of their respective ethnic causes. While each of them looks at ethnicity from a different perspective, the ideas of ethnicity and racism pervade their writings. The basic purpose of all these novels under discussion is to show the conflict between an ethnic group and the dominant European Americans. The racial conflict arises because of several factors. The most prominent factor being the assimilation factor, from the point of view of the ethnic groups and the acceptance factor from the point of view of the larger European American Society. Each of the three novelists treats this problem differently. There has also been a great degree of variation in the magnitude of ethnic awareness in these writers. In case of Bernard Malamud, the Jewish ethnic awareness is prominent but the protest against the European Americans is mild. So his is a *voice of resignation*. In Richard Wright's case the tone of ethnic awareness is very assertive and his protest against the larger American Society is highly vocal and assertive. So, his is a *voice of affirmation*. In Silko's writings, the tone of ethnicity is very candid and straightforward. She openly attacks the European Americans for having encroached upon their land and contaminating their Native American culture. But, she is very hopeful of regaining what they have lost. So, hers is a *voice of optimism*. All these three writers seem to have accused the larger American Society dominated by the European Americans because of their belief in racial discrimination. The idea of ethnic awareness is common to all these novels though it varies in degree but not in kind. My book also aims at contesting the traditional notion of America as a "Melting pot" of different races. My attempt would also be to contradict this notion and to show that American society is not in reality a melting pot, but a "Cultural Mosaic" of different races and communities as manifested in American ethnic literature. They enrich not only the mainstream American literature but also the American ethnic literature in particular.

2

Bernard Malamud: A Voice of Resignation

They suffer because they are Jews (*The Assistant* 106).

Jewish-American literature is now only about one century old if we include that literature which was written in Yiddish by immigrants between 1885 and 1935. Yiddish, however, is hardly used in America at the beginning of the 21st century so that anything foreign except some of the works of Goethe and Voltaire has no influence on the American Jew simply because he cannot read it.

Yiddish writers were commonly radicals and secularists. From the time of the first volume of Yiddish poetry published in America in 1877 to the end of the Yiddish era in about 1975, Jewish-American writers always exhibited a strong interest in radical and secular ideas. Yiddish writers expressed themselves in poetry, in the theater, in novels, in newspapers and in intellectual books, papers and pamphlets. The first Jewish novels written in America were written by immigrants. This was true not because there were no Jews here before the last two decades of the nineteenth century, but because those Jews who had come here before 1881 were very few, had arrived in the 17th century from Spain and Portugal and in the nineteenth century from Germany and had rapidly assimilated into the majority American culture. However, 1881 marked a major turning point in Jewish history. On March 1 of that year the Russian Czar, Alexander II, was assassinated. When his son Alexander III ascended the Russian throne, persecution of the Jews became the policy of the Russian government and led to the prompt immigration of millions of Jews to America. These millions of Jews spoke Yiddish so that it is not at all surprising that the first American Jewish writers included in that migration wrote in that language.

Thus, the Jewish writers of that day brought European Jewishness to America. Among these was Morris Winshevsky, who promoted socialism but had very little Jewish content in his poetry. Instead, Winshevsky was a follower of the Jewish enlightenment, called *Haskalah,* a movement with a distinct secular emphasis. In fact, Winshevsky represented the revolt against religion at the end of the 19th century when he wrote: *"For me....my disbelief and hatred toward all faiths reached a high point of fanaticism.....My greatest delight was to prove that Moses did not write the Pentateuch, that Joshuah did not cause the heavens to stand still."*

There were of course, innumerable other authors but only a few stand out as major contributors to Yiddish writing in the U.S.A. There was Morris Rosenfeld, prime representative of the so-called "sweatshop" poets, who reflected the Jewish radicalism of his day. That radicalism was the reaction to the misery of living in immigrant slums, of the exploitation of the Jewish workers, and the desperation of the Jewish masses. It was a radicalism which rejected the religion of Europe and sought to rely on the politics of this world instead. Although Rosenfeld was translated into English, his following in the English language was only temporary so that his fame rests finally on the Yiddish following he was able to attract. He too was an agnostic.

The most important Yiddish writer of the early twentieth century, however, was Abraham Cahan. Although he spoke Yiddish better than English, Cahan succeeded in publishing The *Chosen People* and *The Rise of David Levinsky* in English in 1917. This book has been called *"the most important novel written by a Jewish immigrant"*. In it Levinsky becomes an American millionaire at the cost of his Jewish heritage and upon first becoming a thoroughgoing secularist. "Spencer and Darwin replace the Torah, Dickens and Thackeray the Talmud." Cahan depicts the emptiness of Levinsky's life despite his rise to money and fame.

Other American Jewish writers who wrote in the Yiddish or the English idiom were Sidney Nyburg, Anzela Yezierska, James Oppenheim, Samuel Ornitz and Ludwig Lewisohn, who was born in the United States, the son of German Jewish immigrants. All these dealt with the fate of the immigrants. All of these rejected religion and sought to show how pragmatism and realism were far superior in solving man's problems than belief in anything supernatural.

During the depression of the 1930's American Jewish writers, now mostly born in the U.S.A., were very much affected by the discontinuity of European Judaism with American Judaism. Except for the 1978 Nobel Prize winner in literature, Isaac Bashevis Singer, who was born in Poland in 1904, these writers all wrote in English. Singer, although he wrote in

Yiddish, was published in English so that his work is known to almost all Americans in the latter idiom.

Except for Ludwig Lewisohn and Meyer Levin, who defended Jewishness if not Judaism, these writers all rejected Jewish tradition. Instead, these writers leaned toward the political "left" and viewed their Jewishness as a secular condition. Nelson Algren in *Somebody in Boots,* Albert Halper in *The Foundry,* Isadore Schneider in *From the Kingdom of Necessity* and many others viewed socialism as the answer to the Jewish problem both here and abroad and disdained religion entirely. Demanding a future free of tradition, writers such as Michael Gold in *Jews Without Money,* or Charles Reznikoff in *By the Waters of Manhattan* all believe that Marxism, not Judaism, is the inevitable answer to the degradations and hardships of the immigrant slums.

The writer Paul Goodman, whom the historian Irving Howe called a "Jewish intellectual alienated to the point of complete reduction," thought that the fellowship of all humans is enhanced by the Jewish tradition and that the fully Jewish is regarded as the fully human. Judaism as a religion or as a separate experience is hardly credited by Goodman.

Added to these novelists, there were in the first part of the 20th century Jewish theologians who also strove to distance theology from the European tradition. Kaufman Kohler, a reform Rabbi wrote *Jewish Theology Systematically and Historically Considered* in 1918 and in 1934 Rabbi Mordecai Kaplan, a representative of the conservative movement in Judaism, published his monumental *Judaism as a Civilization.*

Not only did these rabbis disconnect American Judaism from European Judaism, they also redefined the God concept. Thus, Kaplan presents God as "a chronologically variable social idea," or as a "struggling ordering force of nature."

Thus, after the Second World War, *i.e.*, after 1945, a vast number of Jewish - American writers inundated the literature of the United States and have kept this up until the beginning of this century.

A list of all the American - Jewish writers who have contributed to American literature since 1945 cannot be presented here. It is far too long and would involve a discussion of a whole social movement with far reaching consequences for American culture. Some of the most prominent names among American-Jewish fiction writers are of course Saul Bellow, Bernard Malamud, Tillie Olson, Grace Paley, Cynthia Ozick, Herbert Gold, Joseph Heller, E.L. Doctorow, Stanley Elkin, Hugh Nissensen and Phillip Roth.

The works of Phillip Roth are undoubtedly excellent examples of the rejection of traditional Judaism already exhibited by the Yiddish writers a generation earlier. Like their non-Jewish contemporaries and predecessors, Jewish writers in the last half of the 20th century contributed a great deal to the secularization of America and Jewish life as well as they created a distinction between Judaism and Jewishness which their grandparents never knew and which has become the Great Divide within the Jewish community in the twenty-first century.

In 1933, when Phillip Roth was born, mass immigration to the United States had come to an end and Jewish immigration, mostly from Germany, was small and involved many newcomers already secularized by their German environment. Numerous Yiddish writers and the philosophical, scientific and literary world in America had secularized at least the academic world and in particular such institutions as the University of Chicago, where Roth was a student and where American sociology was created.

Like thousands of other Jews who came of age in the 1930's, Roth entered into the world of higher education where the challenges to Judaism or any religion were already embedded in the curriculum. And since over eighty percent of Jews of college age attend an institution of higher education and have done so for half a century, they, like Roth, found every reason to divorce Judaism from Jewishness and discard "the faith of our fathers."

Many of the Jewish writers, with Roth in the forefront, opposed their Jewish heritage and treated it with contempt, disdain and calumny. In fact, since Roth wrote *Good-Bye, Columbus* in 1959 "there are those who still grit their teeth, hoping that the irreverent, satirical Mr. Roth will go away."

Roth, of course, did to the Jewish world what non-Jewish writers had already done to the Christian world for a century. He secularized the sacred. He ridiculed the divine. He insulted the tradition and he vulgarized his "in-group." Thus, Roth, and so many other Jewish - American writers, contributed mightily, not only to the secularization of Judaism and America in general, but also to the de-mystification of the Jewish tradition. This means that both for non-Jews and for Americans of Jewish origins who had left the tradition behind, Roth provides insight into 20th and 21st century Jewish life as it is lived each day. He explains what is important to contemporary American Jews. He shows that Judaism is not one of the important ideas in the lives of American Jews but that Jews have substituted membership in clubs and organizations for membership in synagogues. Roth further claims that synagogues and rabbis are themselves secular institutions at the end of the 20th century, that Jewish ritual emphasizes financial display as in Bar Mitzvahs and weddings and that the Jewish community in America is governed by the same type of business interests which Sinclair Lewis described governing the Christian community exhibited and shown over and over again in *Babbitt.*

No doubt it is *Portnoy's Complaint,* however, which Roth wrote in 1969, that led to the accusations that Roth is a Jewish anti-Semite, a self hater and a self promoter. This book, which attacks the stereotypical Jewish mother, recites at length and in detail the sexual problems of the protagonist. It has been labeled "pornographic" for good reason and was truly "shocking" on first coming to public attention. Now, at the beginning of the century, nothing else will shock anyone any more. Dreiser and Lewis and their companions also shocked Americans. But by the time Roth began to write, the only means of gaining the readers' attention among all the competing writers was to do something yet more extreme than what had already been done before the Second World War. Merely proclaiming one's disbelief in orthodox theology was no longer necessary since, as we have seen innumerable writers in philosophy, science and literature had already made secularization a most popular attitude. Roth and his contemporaries, particularly his Jewish companions, sought to now attack the core of Jewishness as they understood it. This Jewishness, in the hands of these writers, consists of being "raving hysterics", nagging "Jewish mothers", and female shrews of every variety. Thus, the popular Jewish writers in the tradition of Roth were accused of being Jewish "anti-Semites", producers of filth and self - hatred and conveyors of the same calumnies which the Jews of the old world endured for so long.

Roth has rejected all of these complaints in an essay he wrote for *Commentary* in 1963. Roth argues there that his Jewish characters, who are inevitably less than admirable, are never meant to represent all Jews or even a large number. To Roth, each story he wrote refers only to the one person described and without any further implications. Yet, Roth himself quotes a letter he received after the publication of his story "Defenders of the Faith," which says in part.".......With your one story, 'Defenders of the Faith', you have done as much harm as all the organized anti-Semitic organizations have done to make people believe that all Jews are cheats, liars and connivers." Roth writes that he was even accused of legitimizing the murder of six million European Jews by stories which, he does not deny, vilify Jews. Yet, his argument is that those who see these things in his stories do not understand them and that it is submission to anti-Semitism to *not* write about subjects which depict Jews as human beings, *i.e.*, sinners, fools, adulterers, cowards and connivers.

Now Roth has always argued that fiction and reality are different. He did so again in 1987 in *The Counterlife* and seeks thereby to escape responsibility for what are clearly attacks on Jewishness and Judaism. To Roth, Jewish identity cannot be taken for granted. It is always in question as seen once more in his relatively recent effort called *Operation Shylock (1993)*.

Roth holds that it is "timidity and paranoia" for American Jews to object to his stories about Jewish failure and Jewish moral weakness. He will not accede to the common Jewish view that a Jew must never talk about negative Jewish traits to non-Jews. Roth rejects that anti-Jewish conduct can result from his negative stories about Jews. Referring to a complaining rabbi, Roth writes: "Can he actually believe that on the basis of my story anyone is going to start a pogrom, or keep a Jew out of medical school, or even call a Jewish school child a 'kike'?"

Although it is indeed true that one author cannot provoke a "pogrom" it is also true that those who like to set quotas on Jews in medical schools or call children ethnic names can easily feel themselves justified in that kind of persecution by using a story by Roth.

More important is that Roth and his followers have legitimized the distancing of Jews from Judaism and the Jewish tradition and have in that sense contributed immensely to the secularization of Judaism in the United States.

This may be said of Roth despite the fact that in "Eli the Fanatic" Roth exposes the boorishness of many modern American Jews who find even the survivors of the Holocaust irrelevant in their anxiety to avoid being identified with Jews dressed in the black garb of the Chassidim and speaking with a distinct accent.

This then leads us to consider one more aspect to American - Jewish writing which is unique to Jews and has been very influential in promoting secularization in the Jewish community at the end of the twentieth century. That is the fiction and the historiography of the holocaust. This writing has led to the phenomenon in the Jewish community of literally substituting holocaust memorial activities for Judaism so that for many otherwise utterly secular Jews ceremony and ritual surrounding the holocaust has become their religion. This phenomenon was instigated by holocaust writers: fictional and non - fictional. The second way in which holocaust literature has influenced secularization is raised by those who question whether a God can exist in a world which permits such horrors.

Foremost among these writers is Elie Wiesel. Although of a Yiddish speaking background, Wiesel has made a name for himself in both French and English. When "Night" was first translated from the French and published in America in 1960 it opened the door to a wide range of such literature thereafter.

It is true that Chaim Grade had already published "My Quarrel with Hersh Rasseyner" in 1951, but that book was written in Yiddish and only later became available in English. Grade deals with one question in his book. The question is: "How can one believe in God after the Holocaust?" Grade renounces religion and belief in God. Saul Bellow, however, in *Mr. Sammler's Planet* describes in detail the horrors of the Holocaust experience but reaches the conclusion that God does exist and *"nihilism is denied."*

Many Jews have answered Grade's question by renouncing traditional religion and placing their emotions into "holocausting", which refers not only to attendance at various commemorative events, but also refers to financial contributions to the Washington D.C. holocaust museum, the Los Angeles based "Wiesenthal Center," and other such efforts to remember the mass murders of the Second World War. This means in practice that it is much easier for commemorative organizations to raise money concerning the past than it is for Jewish educational institutions to raise funds for the propagation of Judaism among the young.

Jerzy Kosinski in *The Painted Bird,* Bernard Malamud in *The Fixer,* and Saul Bellow's aforementioned *Mr. Sammler's Planet* all deal with the issue of how the immigrant survivor can deal with his past and his future.

There are many more Jewish-American fiction writers who have concerned themselves with the Holocaust. The work of Cynthis Ozick, Hugh Nissenson, Richard Elman, Zdena Berger, Norma Rosen, Isaac B. Singer, Joshuah Singer and Daniel Stern are only a small example of all that has been written and is still being produced concerning that heinous crime.

There is also an ever growing non-fiction literature concerning the Holocaust. Best known among these is Lucy Dawidowicz, who has received the most attention among historians for her book *The War Against the Jews, 1933-1945* (1975) although Nora Levin, writing in *The Holocaust* in 1968, was far more detailed in her description of the events collectively so labeled than was Dawidowicz. There is also the book by Hilberg called *The Destruction of the European Jews* and more recently *The Holocaust* by Gilbert.

In addition to these major histories there are innumerable other works dealing with the holocaust such as oral histories, psycho-social analyses, memoirs and diaries. This literature is increasing as the years since that crime go on. Each of these many publications raises the questions anew. Is there a God? Is religion meaningless? Can one be a Jew by showing an interest in that terrible Jewish experience? The memorializing of the holocaust has yet one more dimension for the vast majority of American Jews who never experienced those horrors. It gives the Native American Jewish population a pseudo-martyr status. American Jews, fortunately ignorant of what is really meant by the word "Holocaust" and not really willing to listen to the first hand accounts of survivors, enjoy the victim status when these nightmares are discussed in public. This kind of stance is evident during the large Holocaust commemorations which secular American Jewish "leaders" like to stage in full view of television cameras and other media coverage. These events are generally chaired by some one known as a "great contributor." Such a personage addresses the crowd and the cameras and creates the impression, at least in his eyes, that he is somehow a victim. In the victim oriented American society at the beginning of the 21st century, this stance is sought after and prestigious and achieved by making large financial contributions. All that in face of living holocaust survivors who, by reason of their general poverty, are often ignored because they have neither the education nor the finesse to make a convincing television appearance. Thus, even the Holocaust and all that implies has become banal and absurd in the hands of those who cannot understand that such overused phrases as "the Jews went to their deaths like sheep" are false and nonsense. Even worse is the effort on the part of some native American Jews, and a good number of non-Jews, to trivialize the Holocaust by comparing it to the bombing of Dresden, the use of the atomic bomb on Hiroshima and Nagasaki or the innumerable slaughters that have taken place since 1945 in every part of the world. All of that is the consequence of the perceived need to compete for victim status in a world so secularized that even the most incomprehensible of human experiences is categorized as an occasion to gain status and prestige.

The American Jewish writers who earlier had to grapple with the problems of defining themselves in terms "Americanness" and "Jewishness" finally found in Bernard Malamud their spokesman for whom the Jew becomes a natural symbol for the postwar sensibility. The Jews in the novels of Malamud emerge as a type of metaphor both for the tragic dimension of anyone's life and for a code of personal morality. Bernard Malamud and a host of other postwar American-Jewish writers had to discover the boundaries of a heritage that, for them, had hardly lived at all. However, the idea of holocaust remained a troubling subject for the American Jewish writers. Though Malamud has been classified as a Jewish-American writer, he objects to the label by saying:

> I'm an American, I'm a Jew, and I write for all men.... I write about Jews, when I write about Jews, because they set my imagination going.... Sometimes I make characters Jewish because I think I will understand them better as people, not because I am out to prove anything.... I was born in America and respond in American life to more than Jewish experience. I wrote for those who read (Stern 56).

Malamud considered his writings to be universal and upheld the view that anyone sensitive to fiction could understand his work and feel it. It is not necessary for a reader to be Jewish or of any particular race or nationality to grasp the subtleties in the writing of a good author, even if that author focuses on a small and perhaps esoteric group. Malamud's attitude towards the Jews and humanity can be briefly stated in the following words as pointed by Robert Ducharme in his book titled *Art and Idea in the novels of Bernard Malamud*: "the Jew is humanity under the twin aspects of suffering and moral aspiration. Therefore any man who suffers greatly and also longs to be better than he is, can be called a Jew" (93).

Malamud presents particular aspects of Jewish belief, history and culture in *The Fixer, God's Grace,* and in many of his short stories. These are usually only the means to an end, giving his fiction what Isaac Bashevis Singer calls "an address". In his novel *The Tenants,* Malamud deals with a problem directly relevant to the Jews in modern America: the black-Jewish conflict of the late 1960s, but even in that book, the protagonist Lesser is Jewish by birth only; he does not show any attachment to Judaism or to Jewish culture. Rather than representing the Jews or in his case, even all men, Lesser shows forth aspects of the artist and his problems with the dichotomy of art and life. This chapter would make an in-depth study of three novels of Bernard Malamud, namely, *The Assistant, The Fixer* and *The Tenants* as these three novels are directly concerned with the theme of ethnicity and my attempt would be to bring out Malamud's response to the problem of ethnicity as reflected in these novels.

The Assistant contains a strong Jewish theme. Throughout the novel, Malamud uses the image of the Jew and the principles of Judaism. The main characters, Frank Alpine and Morris Bober exemplify the basic values of the novel. Frank is shown to be imbibing "Jewish" values from Morris and with Morris' death, Frank replaces him both in the store and in terms of having become an ethnical man. At the end of the novel, Frank circumcises and becomes a Jew, although in the metaphorical manner in which Malamud uses the term, Frank had already become one.

Judaism, according to Morris, refers to a broader aspect of life. He speaks to Frank: "This means to do what is right, to be honest, to be good. This means to other people. Our life is hard enough, why should we hurt somebody else?" (*The Assistant* 106). The point is that although Morris may define Jewish Law as the Torah, the basic principles that he chooses to live by, are universal. Most of the laws of the Torah are universal, but there are many, which Morris chooses to ignore that are directed particularly to the children of Israel. Morris' Jewishness is starkly contrasted with the values of modern America. Indeed, those values are seen as diametrically opposed to the traditional Jewish values for which Morris stands. Honesty and integrity do not lead to success in America, where the possession of money confers a status beyond material wealth. Thus Julius Karp, Morris' successful liquor store-owning neighbor, feels no compunction in lecturing Morris about worldly things.

The central irony in *The Assistant* lies in the fact that Morris considers himself a failure: that is, he accepts the judgment of Julius Karp, who represents the American ethic that monetary and business success are all that matter, even though Karp himself may be aware of Morris' deeper qualities. The irony moves into paradox when we realize that Morris' failure is his success. It is because of his inability to succeed in the American business world, Morris is considered to be a moral and ethical success. He realizes enough to detest Karp's values but wishes that America were the sort of place where morality could lead to practical success. Just before his death, Morris thinks, "I gave away my life for nothing. It was the thunderous truth" (*The Assistant* 193). After his death he was buried "in an enormous cemetery - it went on for miles - in Queens" (*The Assistant* 193). Ida and Helen think that although Morris was good, he was a failure, "He made himself a victim. He could, with a little more courage, have been more than he was" (*The Assistant* 196).

The Assistant is a strong condemnation of American values, because the good and the decent people are not honored by the society. In *The Assistant* it is Frank

Alpine, who most benefits from Morris' example and who carries the metaphoric idea of Jewishness to new areas beyond Morris' definition. Even more than Morris, Frank is the primary protagonist of the novel and the novel is named after him. His attitude towards the Jews and Jewishness was negative in the beginning of the novel.

But there are also early hints of Frank's potential. Although he is not an observant Roman Catholic, as Morris is not an observant Jew, he still appreciates what Morris stands for and practises in real life: his ability to endure suffering and yet remain moral. Frank thinks that Morris' Jewish tradition must be at the root of his actions, but Malamud makes it clear that any humanistically oriented philosophy can have the same effect.

Helen Bober, daughter of Morris, is a clear example of a different aspect of American Jewish ethnicity. She stands for the mad rush for attaining immediate material success as promised by the American Dream. To her, Jewishness is the religion of her parents; a burden which she is unwilling to carry in her search for a promising life in America. Helen rates love and happiness very highly and ironically begins to believe that the things that people have in common are more important than those that separate them; that is, she arrives at a judgment of the oneness of humanity through stressing her own individual needs and by eliminating the Torah, whereas her father arrived at the same conclusion through selflessness and an adherence to his particular understanding of the Torah, or the Law. Ida Bober, Helen's mother takes a very narrow view of Jewishness. She is not convinced of the "human" definition of individual worth. Ida reflects the fearful approach to the new world of one who has never been able to become a part of it. Her view of America consists of the little she knows about it and the vast amount of what she does not know and of which she is afraid. She wants Helen to breach the walls of the hostile American fortress, which she was too timid either to conquer herself or to allow Morris to take the necessary risks to succeed in. Her fear has made her a confirmed materialist, and she has taken on the corrupt values of the American world. Thus, she is willing to deceive the prospective buyer Podolsky, and she pushes Helen toward Nat as much for his prospects as for his Jewishness. In the guise of wanting the best for her daughter, Ida denigrates Morris' morality and constantly tries to persuade him to abandon it. Morris wants a better life for Helen too, but is unwilling to abandon his ethics to achieve it. Morris' view of Jewishness as love and responsibility for all humanity is alien to Ida.

In *The Assistant*, the store acts as a symbol of misery for Morris as mentioned in the text, "In a store you were entombed" (*The Assistant* 3). The store is Frank's monastery and his tiny Spartan room, a cell, "as Frank begins to take on the virtues of Bober, the cell becomes a place of monastic illumination. Each act of suffering for Bober and the rest of mankind strips away Frank's worldliness..." (Helterman 50). Thus, physical imprisonment is essential for Frank if he is paradoxically to release himself from the imprisoning forces within him. What Frank requires is the very imprisonment against which Morris raises a set of four walls, which Frank refuses to leave through self-discipline. To achieve this discipline, he must accept the fact that he is imprisoned more by his own character flaws than by external walls. When, towards the end of the novel and literally at Morris' death, Frank becomes Morris both in the sense of replacing him in the store and in taking on his mantle of morality, it is a sign that he has become a new person. In the end, it is Frank, Morris' acolyte and substitute son, who eventually replaces his teacher in the store. By formally becoming a Jew at the end of the novel, Frank illustrates Malamud's point that "paradoxically, a character may become more Christ like as he becomes more Jewish" (Helterman 2). Whether Jewish or Christian, it is the heart that counts. The transformation of Frank is evident. The man who climbs out of the grocer's grave though looks like Frank Alpine is really Morris reborn, a new Morris who will complete his mentor's life: "Frank will see to Helen's education, one purpose of which is to give posthumous meaning to the grocer's pathetic life. Thus each life gains meaning by what it gives to the next, and the divine circle of the Law, of doing for others, curves back on the point of its origin: the meaning of Morris Bober's life" (Field and Field, eds. 164).

Helen's role in Frank's redemption, in his becoming a moral individual through responsibility and selflessness and concomitantly his achieving a sense of God, is not as important as Morris', but she has some importance in this process. Malamud's depiction of their relationship can also be seen in terms of Buber's philosophy: "when a man loves a woman so that her life is present in his own, the You of her eyes allows him to gaze into a ray of the eternal You. But if a man lusts after the 'ever repeated triumph'-you want to dangle before his lust a phantom of the eternal?"(Buber 154) From climbing up the airshaft to look at Helen naked in the bathroom Frank moves toward a feeling of love for her. He does rape her, however, and one may question Malamud's treatment of this as a sign of Frank's starved love and a result of Helen's having wrongly rejected him. However, unlike Frank, Helen is depicted as a character that does not really grow in understanding. Frank wonders whether she learned anything from the great literature she has read. The rape marks a turning point for Frank after which all the previous events coalesce in a determination, finally to take control of his life: "the wrong he had done her was never out of his mind. He hadn't intended wrong, but he had done it; now he intended right" (*The Assistant* 157). Love replaces lust, and seeing the eternal "You" becomes a possibility. The question arises as to the price Malamud exacts for Frank's redemption. Philip Roth thinks that the price is too high and the method by which this redemption is achieved is unjust. Frank has chosen entombment as being necessary for his redemption; he is a prisoner in the store, slaving his life away for Ida and Helen. Also, he gets himself circumcised; an act of self-punishment to atone for Helen's rape as well as a ritual for conversion to Judaism as we see in the text that "the pain enraged and inspired him' (*The Assistant* 210). While Roth stresses the pain, Malamud stresses the inspiration; the inspiration derived from Frank's hard-won ability to discipline his baser instincts. The element of irony also dominates Malamud's treatment of Jewishness in *The Assistant*. The striving of the characters to achieve their goals is usually undercut by an opposite character trait that prevents their success or by a result that is far different from that which was desired. Morris' goodness achieves neither material rewards nor respect from his family. While Malamud admires Morris, he is ruthless in not permitting him any satisfaction or fulfillment as a result of his goodness. Even, Morris' burial seems to annihilate his memory as it takes place in a huge anonymous cemetery. Affirmation occurs only through a sense that goodness is worthwhile as an end in itself and through Frank's transformation on account of Morris' example. Thematically, the novel centers round a paradox: Morris' failure is his success. The sustained goodness of his heart in the face of business failure signals his spiritual achievement. This paradox receives emphasis from the contrast between Morris and his two successful Jewish neighbors, Sam Pearl and Julius Karp. Sam Pearl owns only a small candy store but has made enough money while betting on horse races to send his son to both college and Law school. While Julius Karp, who started as a shoe salesman, becomes rich by operating a liquor store in their poor neighborhood, selling a product which Morris refuses on principle to stock in his own store. In this sense, Morris is a Jew in a non-Jewish neighborhood and a commercial failure surrounded by Jewish success.

Frank assumes the spirit of St. Francis and Morris Bober completely with his inordinate suffering. Although Frank is cast in the image of St. Francis, his development reflects the pattern of Jewish history itself. After having served a Jew and his family all his life, Frank turns a Jew himself: "one day in April Frank went to the hospital and had himself circumcised. For a couple of days he dragged himself around with a pain between his legs. The pain enraged and inspired him. After Passover he became a Jew" (*The Assistant* 210). Although the circumcision marks symbolic conversion to Jewish faith, Frank's conversion need not be viewed in its strict religious sense.

The act of conversion for Frank is a matter of becoming a new man and acquiring a new self. Frank's circumcision is a nominal act, which rounds off the new way of life he had already taken up after the death of Morris Bober. Malamud might have intended the conclusion to represent a spiritual victory for Frank Alpine, but the affirmation is riddled with ambiguities. Doctrine plays little part in Frank's conversion; Judaism merely provides him with a practical means of enduring the suffering necessary for salvation. As a Christian Jew, Frank becomes everyman, exemplifying the fundamental unity of men's spiritual needs. For Malamud religion's function is to convey the essentials of the "good heart"; he has little sympathy for the ghetto-minded Jew or parochial Christian. The ending of the novel is satisfactory in the sense that Frank's conversion to Judaism provides an appropriate action to conclude the Jewish theme of the novel. The world of *The Assistant* is a world of contrasts: optimism and pessimism, hope and despair, humor and pathos, transcendence and entrapment, materialism and spiritualism. Malamud's vision encompasses human pain and human potential. He conveys hope through the dual vision of Jewish humor; he captures the bitter reality of suffering and shows the possibilities for spiritual growth through suffering. Morris as an American failed to realize in concrete terms the meaning of American Dream as the path he chose to lead life in the United States was not in line with the larger societal pattern. Morris can be said to be a moral person in an immoral world. Though his life could not be of any significance to his family, it proved to be of immense significance to Frank Alpine. The real significance of the life of Morris Bober has been substantiated by the rabbi at the burial ground when he affirms:

> Yes, Morris Bober was to me a true Jew because he lived in the Jewish experience....but he was

> true to the spirit of our life—to want for others that which he wants also for himself. He followed the Law, which God gave to Moses on Sinai and told him to bring to the people. He suffered, he endured, but with hope. Who told me this? I know. He asked for himself little- nothing, but he wanted for his beloved child a better existence that he had. For such reasons he was a Jew (*The Assistant* 195-96).

Jewishness lies in suffering for one another, that is, assuming an interpersonal responsibility. In *The Assistant,* with its main characters Morris Bober and Frank Alpine, Malamud is concerned with the theme of ethnic conflict as well as Jewish identity. Malamud's projection of the value of Jewishness through the character of Morris is a significant aspect of the novel. Though he is aware of the fact that he suffers because of his Jewishness, he never gives it up and as I have pointed out earlier, it was on the other hand, a source of strength for him. In the beginning of *The Assistant,* the relationship between Morris and Frank assumes more religious connotation because of their two different ethnic backgrounds and it gradually loses importance as it moves towards a more personal relationship. The ethnic awareness of both Morris and Frank which was causing a lot of "differences" between the two, finally ends up with uniting the two characters.

In *The Assistant* Malamud interprets the nature of American Society by taking ethnicity as a sociological model and he succeeds in portraying a nearly accurate picture of the American social scenario in the twentieth century. Malamud, however, does not restrict the locale of his novels to the United States of America alone. He goes on to explore the predicament of the Jews outside the United States as well. He has made a brilliant presentation of the theme of Jewish ethnicity in Russia in his novel *The Fixer,* which is a probing study of the suffering of a Jew, at the hands of anti-Semites in Tsarist Russia, who undergoes untold misery during his two and-a-half year's imprisonment. It delves into the human psyche and evokes pathos most poignantly. It also stands unique in the fictional world of Malamud for its imaginative treatment of history.

The novel is based on an actual historical incident of Jewish persecution: the trial of Mendel Beiliss in 1913 in the Russian city of Kiev for the false accusation of "ritual murder" of a Christian child. The Beiliss case has given Malamud, as Iska Alter suggests, "a way of approaching the European Holocaust on a scale that is unimaginable, susceptible, of fictional representation for the Beiliss case transparently holds within it the core of the cultural sickness around which the Nazi madness grew" (Alter 74). The accusation of "ritual murder" or what is termed "Blood Accusation" has not been uncommon in the history of the Jews. It could be traced back to the superstitious belief of the medieval period that the Jews kill a Christian male child on Passover and use his blood as a spray over their Passover Matzos. Malamud based the novel loosely upon the Mendel Beiliss Case. The accusation speaks of yet another of many injustices that the Jews have suffered in the history. Malamud explores the fictional concerns of the history of Mendel Beiliss in *The Fixer* to depict human misery and injustice. In transferring fact into fiction, Malamud, however, does not limit himself to mere "factual reportage". He seeks the "imaginative fact". In his interview with Haskel Frankel, he explains: "*The Fixer* is not factual reportage. As a writer I seek the imaginative fact. You can't make a thing more real than it is but you can make it seem more real through the imaginative fact" (Frankel 39). Malamud takes liberty in regard to certain facts and turns history into a myth, an endless story to disinvent history. Human predicament is viewed as a metaphor of prison.

Yakov Bok, the protagonist of *The Fixer,* is an agnostic and a free thinker. He feels the misery in the poverty ridden shtetl and leaves his community for Kiev in search of a new life of material prosperity. Out of necessity he conceals his Jewish identity and works in a district forbidden to the Jews. He comes to pay a heavy price for this concealment of identity. He has rescued out of compassion a member of Black Hundreds Organization and subsequently a Hasid. But the acts of compassion throw him into a sea of troubles as his enemies distort the contexts to suit their designs. Yakov is suspected and arrested when one of the Christian boys who chased the old Hasid is found dead. His concealment of Jewish faith confirms the suspicion of the prosecuting officers. Yakov pleads his innocence in vain. In *The Fixer* Malamud presents an accurate picture of pre-revolutionary Tsarist Russia. Shmuel tells Yakov that he is safer in the shtetl, that is, jewish village as the Tsar "does not want poor Jews all over land..." (*The Fixer* 12). In the large cities, Jews are restricted to a few districts. However, it is the poverty and lack of opportunity that eventually drives Yakov to look for work outside the district and to live in an area forbidden to Jews. Yakov is in a state of "unrelieved distress" as he is carried on the road manacled and jeered by the crowd. Imprisoned in the underground cell in the District Courthouse, he realizes and regrets his mistake in concealing his identity: "he had stupidly pretended to be somebody he wasn't, hoping it would create 'opportunities', had learned otherwise-the wrong opportunities-and was paying for learning, if they let him go now he had suffered enough" (*The Fixer* 72). Yakov confesses his "stupid deception" of hiding his identity with Bibikov, the investigating Magistrate for cases of extraordinary importance. He pleads innocence about the murder of the child "why would I kill an innocent child, could I have done it? For years I wanted a child but my luck was bad and my wife couldn't have one. If in no other way at least in my heart I'm a father. And if that's so how could I kill an innocent child? I couldn't think of such a thing. I'd rather be dead" (*The Fixer* 74). Answering the various questions of Bibikov on his personal life and philosophical learning, Yakov sums up his philosophy as "life could be better than it is" (*The Fixer* 79). Yakov fails to understand the reason behind his arrest. He spites the jealous God of Jews. He seems to realize the position of Jews in history: "Being born a Jew meant being vulnerable to history, including its worst errors" (*The Fixer* 155) Yakov curses history, anti-Semitism, fate and the Jews but in the process he gradually grows to understand the fate of a Jew. He thinks that his suffering is due to personal fate, his various shortcomings and force of circumstances. He realizes that in or out the Jew is haunted by history. It is as though a Jew carried on his back, wherever he went, "a condition of servitude, diminished opportunity, vulnerability" (*The Fixer* 315). It is not necessary to go to Kiev, Moscow or any other place for such fate. Yakov accepts this bitter reality. His learning will not free him from the prison, yet he feels that it is better than not knowing at all, "a man had to learn, it was his nature" (*The Fixer* 316). The change that has taken place in Yakov is evident: "something in myself has changed. I'm not the same man I was. I fear less and hate more" (*The Fixer* 319). Yakov's hatred for the Tsarist official is, of course, motivated by his intense compassion for the wronged Jewish community. The novel assumes somehow political undertones towards the end as Yakov's confrontation with the Tsar in his reverie on his way to trial unfolds his militancy. The Tsar pretends to be innocent and neutral: "But I am -I can truthfully say—a kind person and love my people. Though the Jews cause me a great deal of trouble and we must sometimes suppress them to maintain order, believe me, I wish them well. As for you, if you permit me, I consider you a decent but mistaken man-I insist on honesty-and I must ask you to take note of my obligations and burdens"(*The Fixer* 333). He refuses to be pardoned as a criminal on the eve of the three-hundredth anniversary of the rule of the House of Romanov. Yakov finally insists on a "fair trial, not a pardon". Yakov refuses to learn the message of mercy from the inhuman Tsar. He indicts the Tsar for his inhumanity and lack of charity and compassion. "Your poor boy is a hemophiliac, something missing in the blood. In you, in spite of certain sentimental feelings, it is missing somewhere else-the sort of insight, you might call it, that creates in a man charity, respect for the most miserable. You say you are kind and prove it with pogroms" (*The Fixer* 334). The Tsar evades the responsibility of pogroms, calling them "a genuine expression of the will of the people". Yakov does not tolerate the hypocrisy of the Tsar and shoots him with his revolver for the injustice he heaped on the innocent people. Yakov's anger against the Tsar is just an anger since it came out of his intense suffering for no fault of his own. Perhaps he would free the Jews from the atrocities of the Tsar by killing him. It is a positive act of emerging out of compassion for his fellow Jews. Waking from the vision, Yakov thinks, "What the Tsar deserves is a bullet in the gut. Better him than us" (*The Fixer* 334). He is clear in mind about one's role in politics and history: "One thing I've learned, he thought, there's no such thing as an unpolitical man, especially a Jew. You can't be one without the other, that's clear enough. You can't sit still and see yourself destroyed" (*The Fixer* 335). He thinks that without revolution there is no freedom and he recalls Spinoza's saying, "if the state acts in ways that are abhorrent to human nature, it's the lesser evil to destroy it" (*The Fixer* 335). Yakov seems to have won the battle of justice at the psychological level. However, the ending of the novel seems to be abrupt. Malamud intertwines information about the historical setting with that relating to anti-Semitism and Christianity. There are a number of references to anti-Semitic folklore. Before Yakov even enters Kiev, the Drieper boatman says that Jews have "hooves" (*The Fixer* 27), a reference to the belief among the bigoted masses that Jews are devils. A boy follows Yakov, poking his fingers up like horns over his head because the Bible stated that Moses had beams of light emanating from his forehead. Grubeshov tells Yakov that in the middle Ages Jewish men were said to menstruate, a belief still held by some Russians, as the officials are waiting for Yakov to begin to bleed from his penis.

With popular beliefs like these, it is easy to understand how the blood libel could be utilized by the Tsar to suit his purpose against the Jews. He succeeded in manipulating this since anti-Semitism was very much rooted in Christianity. While it may be said that none of Bok's persecutors are true to their Christian faith, it is all too easy to make

Christianity serve the evil purposes of a fearful, reactionary, autocratic regime. Most Christians in *The Fixer* act in extraordinarily un-Christian ways. Malamud relies on the shock of hypocrisy to push home his attitude towards the perversion of religious belief which finds reflection in the Tsarist Russia. Malamud has employed Russia as a metaphor for America in *The Fixer*. His heroes leave one place for another in an attempt to get rid of their restrictive past. Roy Hobbs, Frank Alpine, Levin, and Yakov Bok all fit into this pattern. The problem is, they carry themselves with them, along with those elements of their past which they are so desirous of relinquishing, but the past cannot be discarded. Also, "the desire to escape the past serves as a metaphor for the flights from responsibility in the present" (Ducharme 99). The characters must learn that happiness cannot be achieved while attempting to fulfill only themselves; concern for the welfare of others is also essential for fulfillment.

While *The Fixer* is set within a particular place and historical period, there are many foreshadowing of the Holocaust. Malamud uses the persecution of one Jew to illustrate the societal attitudes that influence such action and which would lead to the murder of millions of equally innocent people. Perhaps this is the only way a fiction writer can come to grips with an event of such magnitude - by focusing on one victim of injustice. Malamud shows that within Tsarist Russia exist all the prejudices held by Nazi Germany, beginning with the ferryman's prediction of the mass slaughter of the "Zhids" and the burning of their corpses in "fires that people will enjoy all over the world.... you can take my word - the time's not far off when everything I say, we will do, because our Lord, who they crucified, wants his rightful revenge" (*The Fixer* 28).

In all his novels, Malamud presents a protagonist who must eventually realize that the only way to achieve self-respect and a measure of freedom is through selflessness and acceptance of responsibility for the needs of others. Roy Hobbs, Frank Alpine, Levin and Yakov Bok all have to learn this lesson. Though he learns it too late, Roy does beat up the judge and Gus and reject the bribe. Frank refuses to accept his fate and uses the grocery store to train himself in selflessness. Levin becomes political in his attempt to change the English Department and takes responsibility for Pauline and her children. Yakov grows in mercy and eventually thinks of others. The inclusion of Russia as the locale of *The Fixer* is to highlight the universal nature of Jewish ethnic issues. As Jewishness is the cause of suffering for Morris, Yakov Bok the protagonist of *The Fixer,* also experiences untold suffering because he is a Jew in a foreign land.

Bernard Malamud's *The Tenants* which appeared in the year 1971 is directly concerned with the theme of ethnic conflict. Responding to the reason of writing the novel, Malamud said, "Jews and blacks, the period of the troubles in New York city, the teachers' strike, the rise of black activism, the mix-up of cause and effect. I thought I'd say a word" (Stern 61).While *The Fixer* focused on a particular period in the history of Tsarist Russia, *The Tenants* treats the issue of black anti-Jewish sentiment in the 1960s, though the Jewish support was there for various black causes.

In *The Tenants,* Harry Lesser and Willie Spearmint reflect each other's prejudices. Even before Willie arrives on the scene, Harry's nightmares contain a black thug that he meets on the stairs. He wonders what it would be like to sleep with a black girl. Malamud presents Willie at times, as a stereotypical black man, one who responds easily to music and actually says: "Don't nobody have to tell me about rhythm" (*The Tenants* 87). Harry's reaction to the white, Jewish Irene being Willie's "sweet bitch", is laden with jealousy, not in the least because a black man is sleeping with her. When Harry and Irene sleep together, he denies it but Irene is aware of the racial implications "...I have this awful feeling as though you and I are a couple of Charlies giving a nigger a boot in the ass" (*The Tenants* 148).

Perhaps even more than Harry, who tries early on to compensate for his prejudice by helping Willie with his writing, Willie is full of bigotry, as he is both anti-White and anti-Jewish. Upon first meeting Harry, Willie refuses to shake his hand. His loss of Irene to Harry hurts Willie's pride, but it is doubtful that he loves her. She is more of a status symbol to him than anything else, because Willie refers to her when first introducing her to Harry as "his white chick, not giving her name" (*The Tenants* 42). As the prestige of a Blackman having a White woman wanes politically, so Willie begins to end his relationship with Irene, refusing to hold her hand in public or to take her to Harlem.

Harry calls Willie a "filthy nigger prick" because "I know you want to hear it" (*The Tenants* 134), and Willie calls Harry a "kike apeshit thieven Jew" (*The Tenants* 134). Each character is aware of what words will most hurt the other's racial or ethnic pride, and this reaches its peak in Willie's violent anti-Semitic stories which equate all that he hates in Whites with the Jews. According to him "the way to black freedom is against them" (*The Tenants* 220). The outcome of this conflict is Willie's epithet, "Bloodsuckin Jew Niggerhater", followed by Harry's "Anti-Semitic Ape" (*The Tenants* 229).

Willie's central concern in his own writing is to express the sufferings of Blacks at the hands of Whites. He feels that Whites are incapable of understanding black experience or black feelings, and so cannot tell anything of use about themselves. Indeed, he feels it is offensive when Whites presume to try to write about blacks. Harry's attitude is that of an artist, a believer in the universality of which art is capable. He tells Willie "if you're an artist you can't be a nigger..." (*The Tenants* 51) and "if the experience is about being human and moves me then you've made it my experience" (*The Tenants* 75). His stress is on the importance of form, which Willie resists as being part of White, not black writing. Willie and Harry frequently see aspects of themselves in each other. Both are struggling as writers to put into order on paper elements of their experiences which they even do not fully understand. Harry lacks Willie's orientation to life, to real experience; Willie needs more of Harry's understanding of form, as when Harry tells him, "You can't turn black experience into literature just be writing it down" (*The Tenants* 74). Each writer becomes the other's victim because neither is capable of a sufficient depth of sympathy for the struggles and limitations of the other.

In *The Tenants* there is a continuation of the prison motif that occurs in various guises in all Malamud's novels. Characters have been trapped by their pasts, goals, mistakes or personality flaws. In some instances a literal structure has symbolized this entrapment, such as the store in *The Assistant*, the cell in *The Fixer* and the tenement in *The Tenants*. The tenement in which Harry and Willie entomb themselves effectively blocks out much of the real world. When the world does enter demanding concern and compassion, as with a whimpering dog with a bleeding eye, Harry immediately removes it from the building, ignoring sounds of "muted cries, distant wailing..." (*The Tenants* 24) that seems to float in from the city outside. The isolation of Harry and Willie in the tenement permits Malamud to focus on them in great detail. There is also a symbolic parallel between the disintegrating building and the state of race relations in the United States. The building may be seen to verge on becoming an objective correlative for the emotions roused by the claustrophobic nature of the protagonists' obsessions with writing and the jungle like ferocity of their eventual confrontations, in which racial issues are predominant. *The Tenants* is an essentially gloomy and pessimistic novel, not possessing even the limited and qualified optimism that exists at the end of *The Fixer*. Given what has happened in the story, the likelihood of the interracial wedding that took place at the end of the novel between Harry and Mary and Willie and Irene is remote. With the possible exception of Irene, none of the characters is particularly amenable to sympathy from the reader. Cynthia Ozick, however, thinks that characterizations are flawed, but not completely so: "The balance was unequal, the protagonists unfairly matched, the Jew too hesitant and disciplined, the black too spontaneous and unschooled" (90). She sees Malamud as reflecting the times, stating that he "did not make Willie. He borrowed him - he mimicked him - from the literature and the politics of the black movement. Willie is the black dream that is current in our world. Blacks made him. Few blacks disavow him" (Ozick 95). Lesser talks about universality but uses his writing for the most subjective, egoistic reasons and a private search for self. On the other hand, Willie, who realizes his writing as a search for identity, egoistically believes that his own identity equals all black identity. Both Lesser and Willie lack insight into humanity and life, a sense of objective purpose, insight into their own past and cultural heritage, and a clear sense of where they stand as individuals or as artists. Willie and Lesser are representative men, microcosms of the nation. Lesser who wants to write about love and truth, loves only self and tells only enough truth to preserve his own false self-image. Willie, who wants to write for black freedom, attaches himself to a White girl for physical support and a White man for moral encouragement, a White man he constantly refers to as "Lesser man". Yet Willie refuses to admit that the souls of the Whites are the same as his own, that Whites do feel as he does, given the same situations, that compassion can be shared between Black and White for either to flourish. In *The Tenants* Malamud plays the legitimate role of a social critic, identifying the social ills, their ramifications and consequences. In the conflict between Lesser and Willie and their foils, Malamud realizes his themes: the conflict between Black and White in the American society, the relationships governing art, life, social involvement, individual commitment, and social obligations.

Leslie Fiedler in the year 1967, observed that Jews were the only White Americans who might feel no guilt towards blacks since they neither owned slaves nor had any part in lynching. Moreover, Jews can see in blacks a people who are treated as they themselves once were, a people who in America have taken on the role of Pariah like them.

Malamud thinks of "*The Tenants* as a sort of prophetic warning against fanaticism. 'The Book', he says, 'argues for the invention of choices to outwit tragedy' " (Shenker 22). When asked why he needed three endings, Malamud replied, "Because one wouldn't do" (Stern 61). It could be argued, in fact, that two more endings precede the three. The first is a reverie, wherein Harry imagines Levenspiel's setting fire to the building, thus providing an end both to himself and his novel. A second possible ending occurs when Willie burns Harry's manuscript, which has been ten years in the making.

The three major endings take place in the concluding part of the novel and reflect the possible outcomes of Black-White relations in the United States of America. The first is apparently hopeful: black and White will intermarry and solve the problem of racial conflict. However, there are many caveats and hesitancies expressed. The Chief says: "when our black daughter marry the white mens we do not rejoice..." (*The Tenants* 210). Shortly afterward he adds: "The ceremony of reconciliation is useless. Men say the words of peace but they do not forgive the other". (*The Tenants* 211-12). The rabbi is equally nervous and "stares in amazement at the assemblage" (*The Tenants* 209), later saying: "My rabbinical colleagues will criticize me strongly for performing this ceremony..." (*The Tenants* 216). The second ending concludes a period in which Harry has destroyed Willie's typewriter, having found that his own paper gave off an unpleasant odor, that of hate. He has had a reverie of being destroyed in another fire, this time set by Willie. He now no longer writes; that is, he no longer attempts to find out about love. The building has become a jungle and each strikes the other in the place where his own group is most prone to being stereotyped, thus showing how much like the other each has become. So, Harry sinks an axe in Willie's brain and Willie cuts off Harry's balls. Like the previous ending, this one is also fantasy;

it does not occur. The only hope is seen in the final phrase: "Each, thought the writer, feels the anguish of the other" (*The Tenants* 230). But, it is too late for this feeling to have an effect.

The final ending of the novel is Levenspiel's cry for mercy. Since the first ending is unlikely, the only way to avoid the second may be through Levenspiel's plea that black and White must have mercy for each other as struggling fellow human beings. While some critics think this triple ending as inadequate, actually an avoidance of an ending, Malamud's provision of choice here mirrors the reality. Malamud admitted in an interview four years after the novel's publication: "It's impossible to predict-it may go one way; it may go another" (Field 1975, 14)). In a climactic scene, more hallucinatory than real, the two writers meet in a dark hallway, transmuted by Lesser's fervid imagination into a primitive jungle, and lock themselves together in a bloody struggle: "Bloodsuckin Jew Niggerhater" followed by "Anti-Semitic Ape". Acting out the last stage of their hatred for each other, Harry cleaves Willie's skull with a razor-sharp saber. The final words of the novel are Levenspiel's: as he discovers the bodies and prays for mercy-for himself, for Lesser and Willie, and for mankind- "Mercy, mercy,...mercy".

Willie and Lesser stand for two racial identities, signifying two distinctly different cultural backgrounds. Thinking of himself almost totally as an artist rather than Jew, Harry considers ethnicity an inadequate basis of art. Willie defines his writing as black writing, which no White can understand. As emblems, the Jewish writer represents a humanistic tradition that strives to advance civilization by using reason to discover the universal truths of human experience. The black writer is a symbol of a black community struggling to create a new black culture. In this sense *The Tenants* is a parable of the black-white confrontation. It pits the notion of civilized White against savage Black, love versus hate, reason versus instinct, Israel versus Ishmael.

A close analysis of the novels of Bernard Malamud suggests that the relationship between Bernard Malamud's literary imagination and his Jewish background has been a peculiar one. In Malamud's work, the immigrant experience is at once more peripheral and more central than in writers of comparable background. Although most of his protagonists are orthodox Jews, he has never really written about the Jews, in the manner of other American Jewish novelists. Malamud clearly means Jewishness to function as an ethical symbol. He is the first important American writer to shape out of his early experiences in the immigrant milieu, a whole distinctive style of imagination and to a lesser degree, a distinctive technique of fiction as well. Writers, prior to Malamud, who had extensively employed Jewish materials, did not usually gain a wide audience. Instead, his choice, as indicated by his early publications, seems to have come naturally out of his own background and the need of every writer to grapple with the experiences of the past. The suggestion that all men are "Jews" can be an appealing idea for Americans. We tend to believe in a moral or spiritual equality even more than we believe in equality of opportunity. For any number of historical and cultural reasons, it is fitting that Malamud has dramatized the Jew as moral doppelganger to the Americans. There is some irony in the fact that much of the prejudice against the Jews in America began not so much from religious hostility, as from the super energetic pursuit of the

American Dream. The stereotype before World War II was largely one of acquisitiveness – Jews will make a place for them; acquire money, and status regardless of the moral cost. This pattern becomes even more alien when we stop considering the underpinnings of the American Dream. Calvinistic doctrine held that the accumulation of worldly wealth was a sign of God's favor. And this doctrine, in turn, was derived from the history of Judaism, the Old Testament. The counter idea that wealth is a source of evil and can destroy character was also carried to this country within Protestantism, having for us essentially New Testament origins, and grew in strength in the Nineteenth century, largely as the result of pastoral Romanticism.

Most of the novels of Malamud are fine examples of the reversal of the American Dream. This reversal provides the real source of power for one of the most impressive novels of the post war period *The Assistant*. Here we find Frank Alpine whose vague ambition to become a glamorous desperado leads him to participate in a stupid and brutal robbery of a pitifully poor neighborhood grocery of Morris. The senseless beating of the storekeeper leads him to a crisis of conscience. Bober, the grocer, is in fact, his conscience. Bober's influence grows over Frank to such an extent that Frank eventually becomes Bober, while gradually casting out the original Frank who was after "American Dream through robbery". In his newly acquired incarnation, Frank ends up with long hours, little remuneration, and almost no chance for advancement while doing service for others. While Frank has not gained anything more, he has become something more.

I have pointed out in the beginning of the chapter that although Malamud always disapproved of the label "Jewish American", his best literary work, *The Assistant* might be called "Jewish" in the real sense. Malamud's concern for humanistic values found its most fruitful expression in his depiction of Jewish characters. The effectiveness of the Jewish characters and their situations is directly related to Malamud's view of suffering. While many groups have experienced unjust suffering, the Jews have had more than their fair share of it in their long history. Malamud frequently uses the figure of the schlemiel, a victim with a comic aspect, to depict the human plight. This figure brings forth compassion rather than mockery and ridicule; pathos is the primary emotion elicited as the schlemiel's situation moves close to tragedy. The schlemiel figure being powerless and pitiable grew out of the ironic situation of the Jews in history; their belief that they were chosen by God for a special purpose contrasted with a daily situation in which they were treated as pariahs. This led to the creation of Jewish humor, which is highly ironic and "capable of sustaining hope while recognizing despair" in its incorporation of both the tragic and the comic.

Malamud seems to have dealt with the theme of ethnicity in the three novels I have discussed from three different angles. In *The Assistant* Malamud depends on the character of Morris Bober to present his ethnic point of view. Morris Bober is out and out a Jewish character who has embraced Judaism to give a direction to his life in the United States. Morris' Jewishness is a source of his strength though it has never paid him rich dividends in the realm of business. Morris could bring about a sea change in the attitude of Frank Alpine just by being with him. That Morris could inspire and influence Frank to embrace Judaism eventually shows the inherent strength of Morris, and by extension of Judaism. Malamud is of the opinion that by taking recourse to the values of Judaism one can lead a life of significance though not of prosperity in the United States. Malamud has finally shown the triumph of Judaism in the novel. The voice of resignation which characterizes the art of novel writing of Malamud is evident in Morris Bober's statement "we suffer because we are Jews" as Morris Bober finds himself in a hostile atmosphere in the United States. Yakov Bok in *The Fixer* also finds himself in an anti-Semitic Tsarist Russia. Yakov hides his Jewish identity in an alien land to keep himself away from the ethnic problems. But he is falsely implicated in a murder case and he comes to pay a heavy price for his concealed Jewish identity. He desperately wants to prove his innocence but that hardly works. He finally realizes the pitiable conditions of the Jews in the course of history. *The Fixer* is a radical novel in the sense that Yakov Bok as a representative Jew thinks of changing the course of history by overthrowing the Tsar although in a reverie. Yakov's growing realization of his self that "there's no such thing as an unpolitical man, especially a Jew" (*The Fixer* 335) reinforces Malamud's voice of resignation in the novel. The locale of *The Fixer* is Russia, unlike that of the other novels, which is suggestive of the universal Jewish predicament. *The Tenants* also brings out the theme of ethnicity in the United States in clear terms. In *The Assistant* and *The Fixer* Morris Bober and Yakov Bok find it very difficult to cope up with the anti-Jewish social surroundings. *The Tenants* offers a peculiar ethnic problem in the sense that the racial conflict is confined to two minority groups: the Blacks and the Jews. Malamud tends to suggest that the interethnic relationships in the United

States society are also not very congenial. It might be a survival strategy on the part of both the minority groups to overpower each other. But the consequence is precarious. Violence only perpetuates violence and there is no end to it. In *The Tenants* the theme of racial conflict is carried forward to the domain of art as both the protagonists are writers by profession. Malamud offers three endings to the novel, which is symbolic of the indecisive attitude of the author as to the solution to the perennial racial conflict in the United States society. Though Malamud suggests interracial marriage as a means to bring this problem to an end, he is skeptic of the efficacy of the proposition. Malamud's usual tone of resignation is evident when he pleads for mercy on the part of both the writers. It is evident that the Jewish characters in all these three novels are victimized by the social forces. The ideas of Jewishness and suffering are like the two sides of the same coin in the Malamudian context. In spite of this, the Jewish characters know how to celebrate their Jewish identities and to derive the meaning of life from a seemingly meaningless world.

3

Richard Wright: A voice of Belligerence

> *...in reality they constitute a separate nation, Stunted, stripped, and held captive within this nation... (Native Son 333).*

Africans were great storytellers long before their first appearance in Jamestown, Virginia, in 1619. The rich and colorful history, art and folklore of West Africa, the ancestral home of most Afro-Americans, present evidence of this notion.

Contrary to a misconception which still prevails, the Africans were familiar with literature and art for many years before their contact with the Western world. Before the breaking up of the social structure of the West African states of Ghana, Melle (Mali), and Songhay, and the internal strife and chaos that made the slave trade possible, the forefathers of the Africans who eventually became slaves in the United States lived in a society where university life was fairly common and scholars were beheld with reverence.

There were in this ancestry rulers who expanded their kingdoms into empires, great and magnificent armies whose physical dimensions dwarfed entire nations into submission, generals who advanced the technique of military science, scholars whose vision of life showed foresight and wisdom, and priests who told of Gods that were strong and kind. To understand fully any aspect of Afro-American life, one must realize that the black American is not without a cultural past, though he was many generations removed from it before his achievements in American literature and art commanded any appreciable attention. Negroes played an important part in American life, history, and culture long before 1619. Their relationship to this country is as old as the country itself.

Africans first came to the new world as explorers. They participated in the exploratory expeditions of Balboa, the discoverer of the Pacific, and Cortes, the conqueror of Mexico. An African explorer helped to open up New Mexico and Arizona and prepared the way for the settlement of the Southwest, Africans also accompanied French Jesuit missionaries on their early travels through North America.

In the United States, the art and literature of the Negro people has had an economic origin. Much that is original in black American folklore, or singular in "Negro spirituals" and blues, can be traced to the economic institution of slavery and its influence upon the Negro's soul.

After the initial poetical debut of Jupiter Hammon and Phillis Wheatley, the main literary expression of the Negro was the slave narrative. One of the earliest of these narratives came from the pen of Gustavas Vassa, an African from Nigeria. This was a time of great pamphleteering in the United States. The free

Africans in the North, and those who had escaped from slavery in the South, made their mark upon this time and awakened the conscience of the nation. Their lack of formal educational attainments gave their narratives a strong and rough-hewed truth, more arresting than scholarship.

Gustavas Vassa established his reputation with an autobiography, first printed in England. Vassa, born in 1745, was kidnapped by slave merchants when he was 11 years old and taken to America. He was placed in service on a plantation in Virginia. Eventually, he was able to purchase his freedom. He left the United States, made his home in England and became active in the British anti-slavery movement. In 1790, he presented a petition to Parliament to abolish the slave trade. His autobiography, *The Interesting Narrative of the Life of Gustavas Vassa*, was an immediate success and had to be published in five editions.

At the time when slave ships were still transporting Africans to the New World, two 18th century Negroes were writing and publishing works of poetry. The first of these was Jupiter Hammon, a slave in Queens Village, Long Island. In 1760, Hammon published *An Evening Thought: Salvation by Christ with Penitential Cries*. ... In all probability this was the first poem published by an American Negro. His most remarkable work, "An Address to the Negroes of New York," was published in 1787. Jupiter Hammon died in 1800.

Phillis Wheatley (1753–1784), like Hammon, was influenced by the religious forces of the Wesley-Whitefield revival. Unlike Hammon, however, she was a writer of unusual talent. Though born in Africa, she acquired in an incredibly short time both the literary culture and the religion of her New England masters. Her writings reflect little of her race and much of the age in which she lived. She was a New England poet of the third quarter of the 18th century, and her poems reflected the poetic conventions of the Boston Puritans with whom she lived. Her fame continued long after her death in 1784 and she became one of the best known poets of New England.

Another important body of literature came out of this period. It is the literature of petition, written by free black men in the North, who were free in name only. Some of the early petitioners for justice were Caribbean-Americans who saw their plight and the plight of the Afro-Americans as one and the same.

In the preceding chapter I have tried to show that Malamud's response to the problem of ethnicity has been that of resignation and a kind of unwilling acceptance as his Jewish characters find themselves mostly as the victims in an alien environment. Their immediate problem is that of survival which they somehow manage to devise and succeed since all their attempts to acculturate themselves into the American mainstream fail due to certain insurmountable factors for which they do not have the answer. The most important hurdle being the anti-Semitic attitude on the part of the dominant European Americans. Morris Bober's statement in *The Assistant,* "we suffer because we are Jews" epitomizes the predicament of the Jews in a foreign land. Another important ethnic group in the American society that has been subjected to a lot of oppression and suffering like the Jews is the community of Afro-Americans. Persecution, pain and suffering are common ingredients in both the Afro-American and Jewish-American literature. Yet, despite these similarities, contemporary Afro-American and Jewish-American literature seem quite different from each other. Studies of Jewish fiction generally emphasize its compassionate and humanistic values;

in contrast, analyses of black literature center on its rage and violence. There was a time in the history of Afro-American literature when there were writers like William Wells Brown, James Weldon Johnson and Charles Chesnutt whose primary objective of writing was to appease the white readers. But, Richard Wright as an Afro-American novelist emerged as a different type of Black writer whose fictional characters develop into rebels and violently attack the society. Richard Wright brought about a radical change in the American psyche as to the position of the Negroes in the American Society. He also questioned the genuineness of the premises upon which the ethical foundation of the American society rests.

Richard Wright has always been a very radical Afro-American ethnic writer whose primary concern has always been to safeguard the interest of his community. He has voiced the bitter feelings of his community in his writings. One of the major concerns of the Afro-American ethnicity has been the attempts made by the Afro-Americans to assimilate into the mainstream American society and the resultant reservation shown by the dominant society towards them. Because the Negroes have found it too difficult to escape from the feeling of racial self consciousness and hence remained ethnic within themselves. Both within the society and outside in its full areas of participation, this enigma of life has provided the necessary emotional conflict for the thematic content of the Afro-American novels. Moreover, here are also numerous factors in the environment which operate against this attempt of acculturation into the American society. The Afro-American novelists have stressed the role of the underprivileged and the dispossessed Negro inhabitants of America in their novels. They have castigated the society for not allowing them to grow fully as independent human beings but to treat them as unwelcome and undesirable intruders.

Preoccupation with the ethnic themes has been the characteristic of the Negro novelists in America throughout the twentieth century. It has become an accepted phenomenon that the Negro novelists write successfully and convincingly only about Negroes. In the Afro-American novels, there has always been a primary postulate that because of ethnic background, Negroes in particular are different from their White neighbors even though both groups follow the same cultural pattern. In the decade 1940-1950, Negro novelists achieved notable success with ethnic themes. Though the theme of rage and violence dominates the major bulk of writings of Richard Wright, his *Native Son* and *Black Boy* have tremendous ethnic overtones and my attempt in this chapter would be to trace the ethnic dimensions as reflected in these two novels.

Richard Wright became the "apostle of race" with the publication of his phenomenally successful novel, *Native Son* which came out in 1940. In this novel, Wright delves into the question of black ethnicity with bludgeoning intensity and explores the different levels of Afro-American psyche. Bigger Thomas, the protagonist of the novel, in fact, stands for his community of African Americans as Morris Bober in Malamud's *The Assistant* represents the Jewish community in the United States. Both Morris Bober and Bigger Thomas are failures in the American Society. But there is a basic difference in the attitude of these two characters as to the racial discrimination being practised in the United States. Morris Bober accepts suffering as his fate and he tries to internalize his suffering but Bigger Thomas becomes violent and rebellious and questions the validity of racial prejudice against the blacks by the white Americans. When he is introduced to the glowing account of American ideals and what they entail, he feels exhilarated. The picture of the American citizen looks very promising to him and he becomes happy to understand that America is unique in its fundamental concept of individual freedom. Here all the citizens are permitted to enjoy the freedom of America and to participate as active citizens. There is scope for everyone to become independent, courageous and happy. Bigger being an American citizen dreams of realizing this ideal but gradually he comes to know that he can not attain the American ideal because he is a Negro. The same society which holds out such an attractive way of life to the American citizens denies self-realization to Bigger. For this reason he asks gropingly, "why"? This question forms the very basis of Wright's writings. The conflicting forces at work within the youthful mind of Bigger baffle him and at last overwhelm him leading to an incurable neurosis. This psychological state transforms Bigger into a criminal whose atrocious crimes astound and horrify the readers. It is clear, from the author's point of view, that society is responsible for what Bigger has become. The only crime that Bigger commits is the crime of being born as a Negro. Yakov Bok in Malamud's *The Fixer* also suffers and undergoes untold misery because of his being a Jew, "his fate nauseated him. Escaping from the pale he had at once been entrapped in prison. From birth a black horse had followed him, a Jewish nightmare. What was being a Jew but an everlasting curse?" (*The Fixer* 227). Across the world the Jews have always been treated as eternal victims. In America the Negro has been the ubiquitous scapegoat.

Scorned by the Whites, and feared by his fellow Negroes for their slavish attitude, Bigger Thomas becomes violent. Even the successful Wright, who has used words as a weapon in his novels was capable of brutality. In his autobiographical novel *Black Boy* which came out in 1945, the author as a young boy rebels against his authoritarian father by killing an innocent kitten. The animal had disturbed his father's sleep and unthinkingly he had told his son to get rid of it. Though Richard realized that his father was speaking figuratively, he enacted the command and reflected that "deep hate of [his father] urged him toward a literal acceptance of his word" (*Black Boy* 10).In the writings of Wright , often animal butchery is a prelude to murdering people. In "Big Boy leaves home", it occurs shortly after a White man is shot. In "The man who killed a shadow" and in *Native Son,* it foreshadows confrontations with the Whites. But in all instances the acts of murder integrate self-defense and release of rage. Richard Kills the kitten to protect himself from his father's wrath but also to "hit back at him" (*Black Boy* 10).Similarly, Big Boy destroys the animals to protect his hiding place and to discharge his fear. By destroying the animals Wright and his characters can express their anger safely and retaliate vicariously against the enemy. *Black Boy* serves as a partial model for Wright's other works in which the protagonists reflect their brutal environments . Although Richard never raised his hands to his mother he defended himself with a Kitchen Knife and razor blades against his aunt Addie's and uncle Tom's attempts to "break [his] spirit" (*Black Boy* 140). Unlike his characters, Wright did not enjoy such encounters and only participated to protect his life and maintain his honor. He blames the Whites for pitting blacks against each other. In one horrifying scene. Wright and Harrison, a black co-worker are urged to box each other for the White employees' pleasure. Although they agree to fake it, the fight escalates into a "battle royal", anticipating the famous episode in Ralph Ellison's *Invisible Man.* Like Ellison, Wright accuses the Whites of manipulating and controlling black behavior and emotions for destroying Negro fellowship. "The shame and anger we felt" Richard writes in *Black Boy,* "for having allowed ourselves to be duped crept into our blows.... The hate we felt for the [white] man... went into the blows we threw at each other" (212).

Richard Wright points out the fact that a Negro, placed in a hostile, White environment which denies him self-realization, throws the burden of responsibility for his crimes of frustration and fear upon the society. Bigger's terrifying behavior pattern results from a special attitude produced by the environment . Bigger, in truth, is forced to play such an unconventional role. In reality, Bigger is a victim of the society and consequently he becomes rebellious. Richard Wright in his article, "How Bigger was born" explains carefully those qualities of his personality which crystallized eventually into the creation of Bigger. In Mississippi, Wright became acquainted with three individual Negroes who, even though unlettered, intuitively resented the role that they were forced to play in the world. Fully aware of the consequences of their acts, these Negroes dared to take their lives in their own hands. They flouted defiantly traditions of White supremacy in an effort to break the stranglehold of oppression by Mississippi Whites in control of the affairs. This control manifested itself in denial of opportunity to the three men. Each in his own way found it necessary to commit a violent crime which resulted in their death in order to enjoy real freedom in that precious moment between death and eternity. Deeply embedded within Bigger is the sincere and honest desire to participate as a human being without the limitations or a set pattern of life which the social order forces him to pursue. Bigger is a composite of the three men. He, like his prototype, is driven to crime by fears and frustrations produced by the society. Richard also makes the relationship of Bigger with White America very clear: "Bigger's relationship with White America, both North and South, which I had to depict, which I had to make Known once again, alas ; a relationship whose effects are carried by every Negro, like scars, some where in his body and mind"(29).

With Bigger there is always a disproportionate amount of fear, an anxiety, which rests squarely upon his utter race consciousness. As a Negro, all of the ideals espoused by men echoing the ethos of the American democratic republic were denied to him or granted grudgingly with emphasis upon the fact that he was a Negro. Bigger is defeated before he is born. Brooding over his plight, he becomes a frightened and bewildered misfit. This leads him in the end to become a violent youth who was eventually eliminated by the society. The Negro problem in the time of Richard Wright in the United States compelled Wright to make of Bigger Thomas a spokesman for the dispossessed, the underprivileged, and the persecuted millions of Negroes who inhabit America. In this way Wright in creating the character of Bigger in *Native Son* strikes openly at the society which produced in him a character like Bigger who does not conform to the generally accepted notions of the solution to the problem. Wright emphasizes the fact that though there were some positive forces at work to redress the miserable plight of the Negroes, yet some reactionary forces backed by the Whites were sufficient to counteract those positive effects. This dramatic indictment of American society is in keeping with the angry thirties which produced Wright and his contemporaries such as John Steinbeck and James Farrell.

Bigger has been deprived of all the basic amenities of life. He struggles to contain his fear and anger, repressing his emotions and establishing a "wall, a curtain" between himself and others. Afraid of "killing himself or someone else" (*Native son* 9), he blots out his surroundings and seeks relief through drinking and brawling. Like a wounded animal, Bigger is dangerous. The taste of blood can unleash savage instincts as revealed in the opening scene in *Native Son*, what Robert Bone observes, foreshadows "the whole novel". The pleasure Bigger derives from crushing the rat's skull is linked to his response to the murders of Mary Dalton, a White woman, and Bessie, his black girlfriend. Although the first killing is accidental and the second is committed hesitatingly, afterwards he feels exhilarated, alive for the first time. In both cases the women's heads are crushed as the rat's skull is. I would like to quote Frantz Fanon in this context who opines that "if the Jew symbolizes the intellectual threat to society, then Bigger , the 'savage nigger' represents the biological threat" (122). Since white America has stunted his intellectual and emotional development, Bigger responds by destroying his victims' brains, the potential source of such growth. The origin of Bigger's psychic state is, frustration based on fear. As a child he has been nurtured in a cesspool of bigotry and often violent human relationships in Mississippi. From infancy he has been taught at home and by the Whites that he is a Negro. At best he must consider himself a little less than a dog. On one occasion in a fight with the Whites, he receives an injury. His parents admonish him strongly not to fight back but to take all the punishment inflicted upon him by the Whites silently. But Bigger's nature rebels against such injustice. When Bigger moves to Chicago, the pattern of race relationships changes in a relative sense. He ponders over his fate and becomes increasingly embittered and ultimately mad. Bigger's mental condition has been shaped by the Whites' ill-treatment of the Negroes for hundreds of years in America. He is a "member of an oppressed race, living in the midst of the oppressors" (Daiches 245), yet cut off from them socially, and in Bigger's case, economically, because he is unemployed. Ironically, Northern liberalism and not the southern brutality has provoked black rebellion. The novel condemns the hypocritical Daltons, wealthy slum landlords who assuage their consciences by "adopting" Negroes, feeding, employing, and educating them in return for affection and loyalty. Ignorant of Bigger's needs and feelings, they treat him as a house pet; but definitely he is not their faithful dog. Instead of feeling grateful, he feels impotent, overwhelmed by the "white mountain that looms over him" (350). When Mary and Jan Erlone, her communist boy friend, pressure Bigger to visit a food restaurant, he finds himself there as an object of amusement and responds to such an attitude with "a dumb, cold and inarticulate hate"(58). Later, after an evening of drinking, he is forced to escort the drunken girl to her bedroom where, torn between desire and hate, he caresses her and then panicking, smothers her. Although Mary's death is accidental, Bigger realizes that he has "murdered many times in his heart" (90). Here, Wright clearly blames the White Americans for creating a creature so hurt and hopeless that only violence provides fulfillment to him. Bigger feels no regret for his act but only pride that "he has murdered and created a new life for himself" (90). His pride is reinforced when he successfully outwits the White authorities by playing the "dumb nigger", a role which allows him to survive . Having killed a White person, he hesitates only briefly before murdering his girlfriend, Bessie, who threatens his freedom.

Wright's characters take recourse to violence because they think that American society has not given them what is due to them. The same is also true of Richard Wright on his personal level. Hunger, fear of a father who deserted the family, the violence of Whites who killed one of his uncles in order to take over his property, the malignity of a "sporting professor" who was courting his aunt and who murdered a White woman with whom he was having an affair and burned the house that contained her lifeless body, were but a few of the grim elements of Wright's early life. There was also the domineering uncle Tom who once advanced on his young relative with a switch: " 'I've got a razor in each hand ! I warned in a low, charged voice. 'If you touch me I will cut you, so help me God'!" (*Black Boy* 175). Violence in the time of Wright was omnipresent. There were sevral instances of beatings by the Whites, Black women raped, Black men fighting back as "bad niggers", Black men castrated and lynched. Squalor, fanaticism and fear characterized the decaying black tenements of southern cities. In such a bizarre scenario the question of survival was the primary concern of all the Black Americans, which necessitated the search for a "survival strategy".

Several passages in Wright's *Black Boy* offer a picture of the black communality, yet the narrator denies the presence of such meaningful relationship in the microcosm that he sets before the readers. There is an almost querulous insistence that his is the only sensitive, artistic, struggling soul in this world. In its projection of a creative soul out of harmony with an oppressive environment, *Black Boy* is akin to the slave narratives. Wright's much debated statement about "the essential bleakness of Black life in America" seems very appropriate. As he has stated categorically, "whenever I thought of the essential bleakness of black life in America, I knew that Negroes had never been allowed to catch the full spirit of western civilization, that they lived some how in it but not of it" (*Black Boy* 45).Ralph Ellison regards this statement as an affirmation of black culture. *Native Son*'s reception gave Wright the confidence he needed to deal with a world he viewed as tempting yet fragmented, and alienating ; in *Black Boy* the intended message is one of transcendence of cultural barriers.

Native Son serves as Wright's warning to White America to recognize her invisible sons before they ruthlessly judge and condemn their country . With nothing to live for, his characters are willing to die for freedom. The more intelligent and sensitive they are, the more they threaten the society. Wright is very particular in projecting the hostile surroundings of his characters which do not allow them to nurture good qualities in them. They are made criminals. The desire to assert oneself in the American society is found in both Bigger Thomas and Frank Alpine. Dissatisfied with his dreary existence, Alpine seeks "adventure and fortune". If he cannot succeed legitimately, he will, like Bigger, become a criminal. He "shivers with pleasure as he conceives of violent acts helping to satisfy a craving that some body suffer as his own fortune improved" (*The Assistant* 78). Since Alpine is not one of Wright's oppressed blacks, he can entertain another vision of himself as a highly disciplined , self-sacrificing individual , a disciple of St. Francis whom he has always admired. Malamud's characters are some-how God-fearing and they do not face the problem of survival in a strictly physical sense. But Wright's characters are always worried about their very existence in the society. The magnitude of the problem of ethnicity is greater in the case of the heroes of Richard Wright than that of Malamud's. Since the society has a step motherly attitude towards them, they are bound to be inhuman. The rebels' actions and attitudes contrast starkly with the victims'. Wright's characters murder repeatedly, yet they feel innocent while Yakov Bok, in *The Fixer* feels guilty for an act that he did not commit . Close to death, Bok learns to appreciate life and to value the limited freedom he once had in the "shtetl". Armed with knowledge and his innocence he can confront the Russian state, demand a trial and proclaim his truth to the world. He might lose his case in the court, but he gains dignity, self respect and purpose as an advocate for his oppressed people.

Both rebels and victims, being part of an ethnic tradition, begin as outsiders in the American society with similar needs for recognition and self esteem, yet they develop quite differently. The rebels fulfill themselves through violence as in the case of the Bigger Thomas and the victims through suffering and sacrificing for others like Morris Bober. In the opinion of Wright , the real criminal is the White American society and the so-called rebel is innocent and his actions are legitimate.

In the novels of Bernard Malamud, I have observed that the theme of ethnicity is directly related to the religion of the Jews , that is ,Judaism. Malamud's

Jews are supposed to be good because it is the right way to live, "My father used to say to be a Jew all you need is a good heart" (*The Assistant* 124), Morris Bober tells Frank Alpine. Richard Wright, on the other hand, in *Black Boy* identifies Negro religion with White repression. According to the White Americans, Black is synonymous with evil and the church stresses man's innate wickedness. The Negroes are forced to believe in their inferiority. In Wrights novels blackness is associated with wickedness. Richard is subjected to unending sermons about his black soul and he has been referred to as a "Black devil" (*Black Boy* 37). Cleanliness of soul, mind and body are stressed constantly but baths and prayers cannot change reality. Richard, being a Black has to carry the stigma for ever. He is made to understand that White society and the black church make salvation possible only in the next life. Wright's characters remain skeptical about a religion which values death more than life. They are in search of answers but receive sermons. Abrupt exclamations and loud declarations stifle any questions. "Don't say that", Richard is warned on one occasion because " God may never forgive you" (*Black Boy* 127).Such religious attitudes stiffen Wright's resistance to the church. Because of this Wright's protagonists view God as an alien, a repressive force but Malamud's characters perceive Him as a partner in a special relationship.

Richard Wright wrote the novel *Native Son* with a purpose. The novel indicts America for its maltreatment of its underprivileged Negroes. It presents the dilemma of over twelve million Negroes in the United States. Life, with this group of people on account of racial prejudice is more difficult than it is with the Whites. Wright insists that unless American Society changes its attitudes toward the

Negroes they will be driven to crimes such as Bigger Commits. Wright places in Max's defense for Bigger's life precisely what he feels that American society has done to Negroes like Bigger:

> The hate and fear which we have inspired in him (Bigger), woven by our civilization into the very structure of his consciousness, into his blood and bones, into the hourly functioning of his personality, have become the justification of his existence.... Every time he comes in contact with us, he kills!... a psychological reaction, embedded in his being. Every thought he thinks is potential murder. Excluded from, and unassimilated in our society, yet longing to gratify impulses akin to our own but denied the objects and channels evolved through long centuries for their socialized expression, every sunrise and sunset make him guilty of subversive actions (335).

In *Native Son* Wright asserts that the Negro race and the Negro Soul lay bare before the bar of White justice. The core of Wright's novel is the insistence upon viewing the conflict between the two racial groups. The perennial suffering of the Negroes in the American Society for realizing the basic necessities of life and the opportunities of the land disturbs our rational process. Recognition of this problem of the Negroes had led to a social change in America. Acquiescence to the idea of change in favor of full equality of status for Negroes became an intellectual conviction years ago, but the application of the principle or formulation of working techniques for making the idea a practical reality, unfortunately, has yet to come in the United States.

Continuing his commentary, Wright asks for the

two minimum essentials for a livable existence in America in positive terms. These have the commonality of aspirations of all people in America as reflected in *Native Son*: "I say, your Honor, give this boy his life. And in making this concession we uphold those two fundamental concepts of our civilization, those two basic concepts upon which we have built the mightiest nation in our history-personality and security-the conviction that the person is inviolate and that which sustains him is equally so" (338). It appears that, Wright's concern for the Negroes conveys the consciousness of the group through Bigger. This consciousness exposes a set of impulses and aspirations that are so fundamental until one must do either one of the two things: to agree to the premise and accept the change of full assimilation or to become emotional at the author's temerity. Biological heritage should be the last thing to debar a person from the fullness of his American heritage. Wright's narrative power and his utter sincerity render it impossible to ignore this Negro consciousness.

Native Son explores the tragic predicament of the Negro community in the United States. This is also the plight of the common man in any social order when he finds, though no fault of his own, that he is doomed. There is with Bigger a brooding sensitivity. Bigger wants to be a human being, to fly a plane, and to be happy. These are ordinary wishes of any youth. But in the case of Bigger, these are denied to him. He attempts to change his environment by adopting an attitude of contempt and cowardly bullying. He is frightened by his knowledge that this fear is almost uncontrollable. He is aware of the impossibility of self-realization in such an environment. In his attempt to arrest the stifling forces which destroy him as a human being, he simply aggravates the situation by committing a crime accidentally, and then he disturbs our sense of propriety and rationality by committing another more fiendish crime. This is not the type of behavior of a youth who has control over himself or adjusted to the world. Finally Bigger meets his tragic end because he resents his frustration, his sense of failure and defeat. If Wright has advanced the premise of the injustice of the Negro, he in turn has also presented and clarified the stand of the majority group. Of course, Bigger is bound to die, but somehow society does not avenge but defeats itself in Bigger's electrocution. Bigger triumphs in death as in the case of Morris Bober in Malamud's *The Assistant*.

For Wright, human values are important in life. In *Native Son* Wright talks about the Negro problem because although it is an American problem it affects ultimately most of the inhabitants of the country either directly or indirectly. Wright's selection of a criminal as his hero rather than an ordinary Negro in his novel makes us aware of the urgency of the Negro problem in the American Society. Bigger Thomas' merciless killing of Bessie with a brick as if she were a rat is suggestive of the seething anger of the black community against the White Americans. His act, though heinous, goes to prove that these people suffer because they are members of an oppressed race existing in poverty for the most part in the land of the oppressors who thrive in wealth and power. The following lines substantiate the prevailing situation very candidly:

> Multiply Bigger twelve million times, allowing for environmental and temperamental variations, and for those Negroes who are

> completely under the influence of the church, and you have the psychology of the Negro people.... in reality they constitute a separate nation, stunted, stripped, and held captive within this nation, devoid of political, social economic and property rights (*Native Son* 333).

For many years the American Jews and Negroes were considered allies in the struggle against discrimination. James Baldwin in an essay titled "The Harlem Ghetto" has analyzed the bittersweet encounter between the two minorities as follows: "The images of the suffering Christ and the suffering Jew are wedded with the image of the suffering slave, and they are one" (67). Although the Negroes have considered the Jews as Christ Killers, they expected the Jews to be more compassionate and sensitive to Black suffering than the Whites. However, Baldwin concludes that America has made it impossible for the two groups to trust each other and to treat each other as equals. From the perspective of Richard Wright and Bernard Malamud, admiration, affection, and attraction as well as envy, hostility, repulsion have characterized black-Jewish relationships. In *Native Son* and *Black Boy,* Wright has depicted the Negro ambivalence towards the Jews, who are both appreciated and resented. In these two novels, Jews provide financial and emotional support to the underprivileged but they are not open-hearted in their attitude towards the Blacks. More pre-occupied with racism than Malamud is with anti-Semitism, Wright does not devote a complete work to show the interaction between the two minority communities but incidents involving blacks and Jews in *Native Son* and *Black Boy.* Despite Wright's limited treatment of Jewish-Negro relationships, it is possible to discern the pattern, which he develops at length. According to *Black Boy*, black anti-Semitism originated in the church and home. Wright observed that antagonism towards the Jews "was bred in Negroes from childhood; it was not merely racial prejudice, it was part of their cultural heritage" (*Black Boy* 54). In this manner, in the eyes of Wright and his young friends, Jews had committed the unpardonable sin; they had murdered the Lord. A ditty sung by young Wright and his friends echoed the sentiments of anti-Semitic White Christians:

> *"Bloody Christ Killers*
> *Never trust a Jew*
> *Bloody Christ Killers*
> *What Won't a Jew do?" (Black Boy 71)*

Wright's ambivalence towards the Jews is developed fully in his *Native Son*. Bigger Thomas resents the Jews who own so many businesses in Chicago's black belt, but he values his Jewish lawyer Max's assistance. For the first time in his life, he meets a White man who seems concerned about him. Helpless, he "felt that he was sitting and holding his life... in his hands, waiting for Max to tell him what to do with it; and it made him hate himself" (211).Although Max is a White he is able to win over Bigger's hatred of the Whites but unfortunately Max cannot truly empathize with the blacks. Because, since culturally and morally he belongs to "another planet" (353), he is horrified by Bigger's rationalization of murder. Like Mrs. Dalton and White America, he is blind to the black rebel's unique sensibility. Although hurt and disappointed, Bigger does not appear surprised when his lawyer gropes "for the cell door, keeping his face averted" (358). Instead, the youth sentenced to death, "smiles a faint, wry, bitter smile" (359), acknowledging that he will die alone as he has lived.

Native Son highlights the differences between the Afro-Americans and the Jewish-Americans which make empathy impossible. Max views Negroes and Jews merely as the victims of capitalism, but he is wrong. While he is called a "dirty Jew" (295) for helping Bigger, the latter is despised solely for his color. The Jewish lawyer chooses to be a victim by embracing communism and its causes; the black rebel has no such choice. With all his education and sophistication, Max is unable to appreciate emotionally what Bigger knows instinctively— that the plight of Black Americans is unique, not comparable to the persecution of communists, Union activists, or the Jews. While both Jews and Negroes may be hated, they are perceived differently by White Christians. In Book two of *Native Son* appropriately titled "Flight", Bigger struggles heroically to escape his persecutors, but he is no more successful than the rat he slaughters at the beginning of the novel. He ends by accepting death which makes it clear that other Biggers will take his place.

In Afro-American fiction flight leads nowhere, as Ralph Ellison suggests in his perceptive essay "Harlem is Nowhere". Usually, the Jewish-American fiction educates its protagonists and brings them home. The contrast is evident in Richard Wright's and Bernard Malamud's works, in which wandering blacks and Jews search for their promised land. Wright depicts the Negro migration from rural South to urban North where oppressive indifference can be as harmful as southern misery. Despite slavery and Jim Crowism, the black community is strongest in the South. *Black Boy* also reveals that communal bonds are absent in Urban areas. Like trapped animals, black characters become ensnared in concrete jungles, and are finally exterminated as the hunters close in. While Wright's rebels are uprooted peasants seeking freedom and opportunity in cities which ignore them, Malamud's victims are ghetto dwellers who, driven by their desire for a better life, leave their homes only to return with a new perspective. As described in *Black Boy*, Wright's life reflects a migratory pattern which began in rural Mississippi and ended in cosmopolitan Paris. A desire to escape the persecution and humiliation caused him first to leave the south and latter the nation. Though he thought of himself as an American and enjoyed her beauty, yet he missed the South and her folk culture which he describes in *Black Boy*. Just as New York City is home to Malamud and his characters, the rural South holds a special place in Wright's fiction. Although the "nightmarish landscape" haunts the author with its scenes of degradations, castrations and lynching, there is another attractive, almost seductive side of the South, a world of morning dew.... wet, green garden paths....dreamy Mississippi water..., of wild geese and sugar cane, and hovering over all the blood-red glare of the sun's after-glow" (*Black boy* 7). It was the natural beauty of South which nurtured Wright and which he was forced to leave but never forgot, as his fiction repeatedly illustrates.

Ironically, the American city, which destroys Wright's Negroes, disrupting their families and communities, sustains Malamud's Jews, enabling them to cease their wandering and establish roots. Culture, history and opportunity give Malamud's city dwellers advantages over Wright's persecuted and semi-literate Negroes. Bernard Malamud's *The Tenants* offers a somewhat realistic picture of the black-Jewish relationship in modern American cities. Set in New York City, the novel explores the interaction between Harry Lesser and Willie Spearmint, a Jewish and a Black writer. The encounter embraces more than two individuals. It is a clash of two traditions; the intellectual and the sensual; a debate between two aesthetics; the rational and the radical. The protagonists enact roles assigned to them by centuries of conditioning.

By the time of his sudden death in 1960 at the age of 52, Wright had irrevocably changed the principles governing African-American writing and had left an indelible mark on the American imagination. Amiri Baraka, an Afro-American writer of repute opined "Wright was one of the people who made me conscious of the need to struggle". In fact, the publication of *Native Son* changed the image of the Afro-American to a great deal. Ralph Ellison was of the view that Wright just did not create his novels but he himself was created by the novels. Wright modeled both his *Black Boy* and *Native Son* on his own life as he drew sufficient inspiration from his experience of being an Afro-American in the United States. Both these novels exhibit the miserable conditions of the African Americans of the twentieth century and Wright holds the American Society responsible for giving rise to people like Bigger Thomas. Morris Bober could not realize the benefits of American dream as his moral standards stood on the way, but Bigger Thomas was not even allowed to chase the path of American dream, as he was not considered to be a true "American" from the White men's perspective. The tone of ethnicity remains very violent in the novels of Richard Wright as the Afro-Americans take recourse to violence as a survival strategy. Wright also wants to affirm that the history of the Afro-Americans is as old as that of the European Americans since both these groups landed on the American soil simultaneously. But the dominant society looks down upon the Negroes as they have had a long history of servitude to the White people. Both *Native Son* and *Black Boy* aim at correcting the attitude of the dominant society because when they proclaim themselves to be the champions of human dignity, they ought to guarantee the same amount of dignity to the Americans of African origin also.

4

Leslie Marmon Silko: A Voice in Search of Recognition

We came out of this land and we are hers (Ceremony 255).

I have placed Bernard Malamud and Richard Wright in one ethnic tradition because of their growing concern for the ethnic themes. In Malamud's case the Jewish characters have been the victims of an anti-Semitic society. Though they do not like the ways of the mainstream society, they lack the courage to voice their feelings against the dominant society. Even, on occasions, when they feel the necessity of doing it, their voice of protest has been very mild. But in case of Richard Wright, ethnicity assumes a violent undertone and his characters are projected as the rebels of the society. His black characters blatantly defy the ways of the mainstream society and they take recourse to violence to assert their position in the American society. The characters of Wright also question the validity of racial discrimination on grounds of color in a democratic society. They want to bring a change in the attitude of the dominant society. They are of the view that black-Americans ought to enjoy equal amount of opportunity in every sphere of the society as with their White counterparts. The Jews feel that they have been marginalized in the society of the United States; the Afro-Americans feel that they are discriminated against or deprived of something and the Native-Americans are given to believe that something of theirs has been encroached upon by the European Americans. This sense of being "taken away" what belongs to them dominates the writings of Leslie Marmon Silko. The problems confronted by the Native-Americans are different from that of the Jewish-Americans and Afro-Americans. Though the Native-Americans are the original inhabitants of the American society they are being looked down upon as an alien people by the dominant European Americans. The predicament of the Native-Americans is akin to the predicament of people living in a colonial set-up. Leslie Marmon Silko has taken special care to articulate the feeling of the people of her own community. Silko was raised on Laguna Pueblo, fifty miles west of Albuquerque. She is from a mixed heritage—Anglo, Mexican and Native—American. Her ancestral house was on the fringe of Laguna Pueblo which was neither quite excluded nor quite included. It becomes a metaphor for Silko's life as it was anchored to the traditions and stories of Laguna Pueblo on one side and with Anglo mainstream on the other. She, however, maintains a balance between the two. The Laguna are one of several Pueblo groups like the Hopi, Zuni, Aroma etc. that are diverse linguistically, but which had in common, a village based sedentary lifestyle where agriculture was quite important. Pueblo peoples also shared a highly structured religious and ceremonial life, and whereas in the dominant society the basic social unit is the nuclear family, for the western Pueblos including the Lagunas, society is organized around matrilineal kinship groups centered round a core of women related to each other by blood.

Before the arrival of the Europeans, Native-America was actually hundreds of Native Americas, a kaleidoscope of ethnic groups, each unique because of its combination of economic organization and technology, language, religion and political values. It is, indeed, a very difficult task to describe with any meaningful accuracy this ethnic diversity. In California alone, for example, there were nearly three hundred separate tribes, each with a distinct identity. The reason being Native-American society was neither monolithic nor highly integrated, contrary to what many non-Native Americans believe. It consisted of hundreds of ethnic groups, each characterized by a high degree of independence and cultural integrity as well as a highly developed sense of tribal loyalty. Most Native-American tribes interpreted life from a certain common perspective, employing a set of values sharply at odds with the assumptions of European civilization. When compared to one another, the tribes are highly diverse, but when all of them are compared to the European society, a Native-American culture becomes discernible, one that revolved around the Native American visions of life, time, community and the environment.

While Europeans placed all things into the fixed and eternal hierarchy of categories, most Native-Americans were just certain that all of the creation—animals, plants, insects, lakes, mountains, rivers, oceans, stars, the sun, the moon, and the wind-had souls of their own. Man is not unique and transcendent but only part of a larger, eternal whole. When Columbus reached America on October 12,

1492, he looked upon the Natives with curious delight, a euphoria based on relief and a sense of fulfillment after a long and somewhat difficult voyage. Convinced that he had reached the East Indies, that he was close to Japan and China, Columbus named the Natives "Indians", a historical misnomer born of geographical ignorance. Unlike black Africans, who came from diverse tribal backgrounds but were forced into a single, highly integrated African American slave culture, the Native-Americans were divided tribally by economic organization, language, religion, and political loyalty. The theologies provided them with a common tribal perspective on the purpose of life and the operation of the cosmos, and the ceremonial rituals became forms of symbolic association in which members of the tribes expressed and acknowledged a common heritage and a common future. Out of common faiths and symbolic associations emerged the religious dimension of Native-American ethnicity. Most Native-Americans attached supernatural qualities to animals, heavenly bodies, the seasons, dead ancestors, and geologic formations. In short, their world was infused with the divine. In a way, most Native-Americans maintained a corporate view of society, even though the intricacies of that perspective made it quite different from the concept in European medieval thought. Intellectually, Native-Americans were carefully bound into communities by history as well as by the oral traditions conveying the past to each new generation. If Native-Americans possessed only vague notions of time in individual terms, they were more conscious of historical time, at least, as it affected their own community. Major events of the past— a tribal move to new territory, a natural disaster, a military defeat or victory—were all remembered. It was the practice of passing on these and other traditions to young people through oral history which sustained Native-American communalism. In the written world of Europeans, where knowledge was visual through the printed page, the individual could independently acquaint himself with the community in the solitude of a library. Indeed, learning could be a solitary experience, simply absorbing knowledge from inanimate books. On the other hand, Native-American views of life, earth, individuality, and community were all merged in their approach to land ownership and it was this issue which lay at the heart of the Native American- European conflict in the United States, directly precipitating most of the violent confrontations. From 1607, when the English Colonists first arrived, right through the controversies during the 1980s, the issue has always been the land with European and American settlers, seizing it throughout the United States and a sincere effort on the part of the Native-Americans to restore it.

As Bernard Malamud and Richard Wright are very much conscious of their respective ethnic traditions, Silko is also a firm believer in the values of the Native-American tradition. Silko feels the necessity of preserving and protecting her Native -American culture in the wake of the ongoing modernization process taking place in the United States. Leslie Marmon Silko, as a typical Native-American writer, attempts to incorporate as many Native-American values as possible into her writings. The present chapter would discuss two of her important novels. *Ceremony* and *Almanac of the Dead* as these novels center round American Indian cultural ethos and highlight the important aspects of Native-American ethnicity. Silko is the right person to have written the novel *Ceremony*. She herself is of mixed-blood and her personal experience has evidently given her access not only to a variety of ethnic problems, but also to a variety of styles of joking. The ceremony, Silko narrates, is that of a Navajo song, but one not sung exactly as it would have been done before the arrival of the Whites in New Mexico, nor sung by a pure blood Indian. As a mark of tradition, the ceremony is to be completed after the song by the sick man, a Laguna named Tayo. His efforts to finish the ceremony by correct action constitute the last half of the novel just as the first half was composed of the events which made him sick. These two series of events, taken together, make it clear that, what the veterans' administration doctors have labeled "battle fatigue" is in Tayo's case at least, is really a struggle for survival. He devises two ways of responding to the attempts made by the doctors to cure him: self-erasure or killing the agent of death. Finally, he is able to find a way to win over the agents of death that will not lead to his erasure as an entity on the reservation, nor allow any one to kill him, and the most important, and not change him too into an agent of death.

Leslie Marmon Silko's Novel *Ceremony* which was published in the year 1977 centers round Tayo, a young man of the South Western Laguna tribe, who fought in the Pacific Islands during World War II. His cousin, with whom he grew up like a brother, is killed by the Japanese. This incident made him insane and when he was supposed to shoot the enemy in retaliation he failed to do that since the enemy reminded him of his uncle Josiah. When Tayo returns to the United States, he is placed in a mental hospital in Los Angels and drugged into senselessness by doctors who are unable to understand his inner turmoil. On his release and return to the Laguna reservation he suffers from horrible nightmares, nausea, and a feeling of total failure. He accuses himself of having cursed the Jungle rain which contributed to the death of his cousin and thereby having caused the drought which ruined the Laguna people. Only after undergoing an ancient healing ritual, Tayo is restored to sanity. He is also made to understand the complexities of individual, social and cosmic sin called witchery and he rediscovers his strong ties to the land and his people.

Ceremony emphasizes the important role that storytelling plays within the Pueblo culture. It also accurately summarizes the repeated attempts of white groups to decimate the Pueblo culture by destroying its ceremonies. Despite these attempts, which began in 1540 and continued until the 1930s, the basic elements of Pueblo myth and ritual managed to survive. As Silko reveals in *Ceremony*, however, the years from World War II to the present have presented new threats to the Pueblos, which, although more subtle than the early Spanish conquests, are even more dangerous, and must be fought if the Pueblo culture is to continue. In order to explain fully the threats the modern world poses to the ceremonial life of the Pueblos, it is first necessary to present a background of the Pueblo geography, basic mythology, and its corresponding ritual. *Pueblo Indians* is a collective term used to refer to the many native peoples of the Pueblo crescent located in the Southwestern United States. This area stretches from Taos in north central New Mexico westward to the Hopi mesas of northeastern Arizona the Laguna Reservation, which is the setting for Silko's novel, is located approximately thirty-five miles from Albuquerque, and about seventy miles from Los

Alamos, where the first atomic bomb was developed.

The three most important figures in Pueblo mythology are Thought Woman, Corn Mother, and Sun Father. While all three beings are extremely powerful, they are also interdependent. Thought Woman is attributed with the creation of the universe, and one version of the creation myth is as follows:

Ts' its' tsi' nako, Thought-Woman,
is sitting in her room
and what ever she thinks about
appears.
She thought of her sisters,
Nau' ts' ity' i and I' tcs' i,
and together they created the Universe
this world
and the four worlds below.
Thought-Woman, the spider,
named things and
as she named them
they appeared.
She is sitting in her room
thinking of a story now
I'm telling you the story
she is thinking. [1]

This myth is important in two respects. First, it explains the Pueblo belief that the universe consists of our world, which is the earth, and the "four worlds below," where the spirits of the dead go. Second, it reveals the crucial function that storytelling serves in the Pueblo culture. Storytelling is more than entertainment or even the passing on of history and religious beliefs to the next generation; it is also a ceremony that acts as a link between the mythical deities and the people themselves, whose ritual life is based on the myths.

Corn Mother, also called Corn Woman, is perhaps the most important deity in Pueblo mythology, judging from the large number of ceremonies devoted to her. She is synonymous with Mother Earth, and represents growth, life, and the feminine aspects of this world. Her role in Pueblo mythology reflects the importance of corn as a staple crop of the Pueblo diet. Because corn and Corn Mother are multivocalic symbols for the Pueblos, the ritual corn dance is performed for one or more of the following reasons: to bring rain, to increase fertility, or to assure an abundance of crops. It is a seasonal ceremony that occurs in the spring or summer, and as a result of the influence of Spanish missionaries, it is usually held on the feast day of the village's patron saint. The dance is understood to be humans' appearance before Corn Mother. It has many variations, reflecting the differences among the many Pueblo groups themselves, but it usually involves lines of dancers moving in a constantly changing zigzag pattern. A drummer and a chorus of chanting old men provide the music. The dancers make gestures to indicate the requests they are offering to the Corn Mother: lowering the arms signifies the lowering clouds, moving the arms in a zig-zag motion indicates lightning, lowering the palms symbolizes rain, and lifting the hands signifies the growing stalks of corn. In smaller corn dances, all of the participants are men, but in larger dances, both men and women participate. When women are involved, they often wear headdresses called *tablitas*. This marking likely symbolizes the special connection that women have with Corn Mother because of their shared femininity.

Prayer sticks representing individual petitions are also offered to Corn Mother, and in *Ceremony*, Silko mentions the regular offering of blue and yellow pollen, which can be viewed as symbolizing fertility, to Corn Mother's altar. Silko expresses the necessity of making these sacrifices in the following traditional myth: An evil Ck' o' yo magician appeared to the people and seduced them with his magic. They were extremely impressed, and believing his magic would give life to the plants and animals as Corn Mother did, they neglected the corn altar. Corn Mother became very angry with her people, for she knew the magic was just a trick, and took away the plants and rain clouds, and didn't allow any baby animals to be born. The myth's message is loud and clear: if the proper ceremonial offerings to Corn Mother are not made, the earth's life processes will not operate as they should.

Sun Father stands opposite to Corn Mother, and is the most powerful creative force in the universe. He represents masculinity and light, and therefore white, the color of pure light, is the most sacred color. Cornmeal is offered to Sun Father, which demonstrates the interdependent relationship he has with Corn Mother. He also is connected with Thought Woman, as can be seen in another myth told by Silko in *Ceremony*. In this myth, a Ck' 'o' yo magician tricked not only the people with his magic, but the storm clouds as well, and took both the people and the clouds prisoners. Sun father went to wake the storm clouds up one morning and could not find them. Because they could not release their rain over the earth, the land began drying up, and the people and animals starved. Sun Father took blue and yellow pollen, tobacco, and coral beads to Thought Woman, asking for her help. She gave Sun Father a magic medicine that allowed him to trick the magician and free the clouds.

The relationships between the Pueblo people and their deities are reciprocal: if the ceremonial offerings are done properly, then their needs are met. If they are not properly carried out, then the people are not fully cared for, as the myth about neglecting the corn altar suggests. Reciprocity can also be seen in the relationship between the Pueblos and the spirits of the animals they hunt. Silko describes the tradition of sprinkling a killed deer with cornmeal in order to free its spirit. This is a sign of appreciation to the deer for giving up its life for the people, and if it is not done, deer will not return the next year to provide for them.

Throughout history, however, the Pueblos have been faced with certain evils that the concept of reciprocity cannot explain. For example, sometimes the ceremonial offerings had been properly carried out, yet there was still a drought, a serious illness, or an unexplainable death. The Pueblos solved this problem by attributing unexplainable evils to witchery. The responsibility for challenging the power of witchery falls upon the shoulders of the medicine man, so when the arrival of the whites to the Pueblo region brought a host of previously unknown diseases, as well as an exploitation of power that was inconceivable to the natives, the medicine man was challenged as never before.

Perhaps one of the most ironic themes in *Ceremony* is that of the United States' relationship with the Native Americans. The history of Native Americans and their struggles with the American government have been incredibly bleak. American settlers attempted to destroy the Native American peoples and use the land for their own purposes. Furthermore, the American government subjugated the Native Americans by forcing them into Indian reservations,

"They see no life when they look they see only objects. The world is a dead thing for them" (Silko 135). The American government did not see the land in the same manner as the Native Americans, and the government possessed the power to use the land for their own means. The Trail of Tears serves as a constant, historical reminder of the mistakes the American government has made.

Furthermore, the relationship becomes even more paradoxical during times of crisis. Native Americans become first class citizens when they are needed. Native Americans were drafted to fight for the country that stole their land, yet they were expected to be patriotic, loyal, and willing to die for America, "They were America the Beautiful too, this was the land of the free just like the teachers said in school. They had the uniform and they didn't look different no more. They got respect" (Silko 42). The Native Americans were respected when they were required to maintain national security and when they conformed to American standards. Such discrimination may lead one to doubt just how fair and just the "land of the free" is in terms of their treatment of Native Americans. Discrimination of the rightful inhabitants of this nation is quite paradoxical indeed, "...an old white woman rolled down her window and said [to Rocky and Tayo] 'God bless you, God bless you,' but it was the uniform, not them she blessed" (Silko 41).

Another very vital aspect is America's paradoxical perception of the Native-American culture. In a sense, Americans exploited Native Americans for their commercial value, such as in the Super Chief railroad lines and the Santa Fe calendars.' Such commercialization was both popular and prevalent, "Josiah used to bring the calendars home every year from the Santa Fe depot, on the reservation these calendars were more common than Coca-Cola calendars" (Silko 121). Furthermore, the Native Americans were also commercialized for their culture and customs, "The Gallup Ceremonial had been an annual event for a long time. It was good for the tourist business coming through in the summertime on Highway 66" (Silko 116). Silko utilizes the cattle metaphor to illustrate how Americans view the Native Americans as marginalized, "Tayo thought about animals then, horses and mules, and the way they drifted with the wind" (Silko 27). In that respect, the Native Americans drift around the country with no land of their own. Americans assigned very little value to the Native Americans, which are illustrated in how easy it was for the Americans to commercialize the Native Americans and their culture. Thus, America only seems to utilize the talents of her native people when a dangerous situation arises, and Native Americans must then risk their lives for a country that has treated them as second class citizens.

The novel is as fragmentary as Tayo's mental condition is and as disjointed as the tribe's position between cultural persistence and assimilation. Past and future are telescoped into the present. The distinctive style of Silko, which is not found in most Anglo-American novelists, is her use of the oral traditions which are intricately woven into the narrative in the form of poems, ritual prayers, stories, and tribal.

In *Ceremony*, Betonie, the part-Mexican, part-Navajo medicine man, educated by the Whites at the Sherman Institute and living on the edges of the Navajo community and the White town of Gallup finally cures Tayo. His hillside hut which is packed not only with medicine bundles but also with coke bottles, telephone directories from various American cities and advertising calendars is suggestive of a process of cultural transformation that has taken place among the Native-Americans in the face of Western colonization. When the Psychoanalysts at the army hospital and the traditional cures of the Laguna medicine men fail to cure Tayo, Silko's hero is restored by Betonie.When Tayo comes to Betonie for help, Betonie explains to him that "at one time, the ceremonies as they had been performed were enough for the way the world was then. But after the white people came, elements in this world began to shift; and it became necessary to create new ceremonies.... the people mistrust this greatly, but only this growth keeps the ceremonies strong" (*Ceremony* 126). Silko, like her character Betonie, is herself of mixed cultural and racial origins and Betonie's biography, the contents of his hut, and his ceremonial transformations should be interpreted not only literally but also as allegorical representations of Silko's effort to create a hybrid literary form, a novel in which Pueblo oral traditions and Western literary forms and narratives are juxtaposed and intercut as part of a complex process of mutual transformation. It is, however, easier to conceptualize such metamorphoses theoretically as an idea than to grasp and analytically describe the actual practice and process of mutual transformation. It is true, as Betonie explains that in Native-American cultures, "the ceremonies have always been changing" (126). Such a view of traditional oral cultures is amply supported by contemporary ethnographic studies and goes hand in hand with Silko's view that any attempt by " the old priests" to "cling to ritual without making new ceremonies" (249) is only a kind of new fundamentalism born out of a fear that paralyses creative response. Nevertheless, it is also true that the kind of changes Betonie makes in the ceremonies and Silko in the oral stories, do constitute departures that are much more radical than those that occur during a process of change within a traditional environment. The reasons for this radical deviation can be understood only if they are seen as responses to a radically new social and political context. This new context is more than the history of contact between Native-American and western cultures; It has been made possible by the unprecedented penetration and disruption of Native cultures by a capitalist political economy since the forties in the shape of uranium mining, atomic-power development, and an atomic-weapons testing program of grotesque proportions. In both *Ceremony* and *Storyteller,* Silko herself is careful to map this form of colonization as an essential context for reading her work. I have pointed out in the context of Jewish-American literature that because of the dominant nature of the European-Americans, the Jews prefer to be confined to a particular geographical segment of the society which gives them a sense of security. The Afro-Americans also prefer to stay in ghettos. That helps them to regulate their lifestyle according to the norms of their racial heritage. The dominant European Americans have always made an attempt to establish an internal colonialism to assert their supremacy in the United States. I have also pointed out in the context of Afro-American literature that centuries of persecution and racial discrimination by the White Americans have made the Afro-Americans social rebels and they have also learnt the strategy to protest the ways of the European Americans.

In the climactic scene of *Ceremony,* the brutal and bloody torture of Harley by Emo, Leroy and Pinkie, occurs in an old disused uranium mine. When Tayo witnesses this scene he suddenly understands that his own mental disorder, the drought that plagues the land, the vision of the witchery explained by Betonie, the disruption of the social life of the Pueblos, and his own persisting confusion of the Native American and the Japanese faces during his service in the war in the pacific, all connect as part of a single historical design when seen in the context of the atomic program:

> And the top-secret laboratories where the bomb had been created were deep in the Jemez Mountains, on land the government took from Cochiti Pueblo: Los Alamos, only a hundred miles northeast of him now .... There was no end to it; it knew no boundaries; and he had arrived at the point of convergence where the fate of all living things, and even the earth, had been laid (245-46).

The mine becomes the point of convergence "in the middle of witchery's final ceremonial sand painting", "a circle of death" that unites all human beings into "one clan" (246) again. In the novel Tayo's grandmother, like some of the older people, still living at Laguna when Silko was a child, remembers waking early one morning and mistaking the flash of the first atomic test for the dawn, a perverse inversion of the sunrise to which the Pueblo people offer prayers. It is appropriate that the climactic scene of *Ceremony* takes place in a uranium mine, for Laguna Pueblo is the site of the largest Open-pit uranium mine in the world. From 1952 to 1981 the Anaconda Company leased seven thousand acres of Laguna land and operated a uranium stripping operation there. When profitably extractable ore was exhausted, the company closed up operations, leaving behind them a massive crater and piles of highly radioactive slag. In *Storyteller* there is a photograph taken in the early sixties looking east form Paguate village at this mine. The mine is a scar, but the familiar New Mexico landscape of hills and mesas still rises up around it. In a note added to this photograph in 1981, Silko points out "the mesas and hills that appear in the background and foreground are now gone, swallowed by the mine" (*Storyteller* 270).

Congenial birth defects and early deaths from respiratory cancer and similar ailments have become more and more common in the mining area. The Laguna residents have discovered that the tribal council building, community center and the newly constructed jack pile housing are radioactive and that Anaconda had used low-grade uranium ore to "improve" the road system leading to the mine and the village. Silko tries to portray the European Americans as "agents of Devil" and their very presence on the American soil contaminates the Native-American culture. The Rio Paguate River, which once provided the basis for a thriving tribal agriculture is now contaminated.

The effect of this global and sacrificial penetration in *Ceremony* is a state in which local cultural codes are either totally erased or radically dislocated and distorted. The bright glare of the atomic explosion reveals to Tayo a world with "no boundaries, only transitions" (*Ceremony* 246). It is the nightmare vision of decoded flows in which Tayo finds him adrift that constitutes the reason for his physic disorder: "he cried at how the worlds had come undone, how thousands of miles, high ocean waves and green jungles could not hold people in their place. Years and months had become weak, and people could push against them and wander back and forth in time" (*Ceremony* 18). The rupture of those codes that map the temporal and geographic dimensions of social existence entails a sense of placelessness, both literal and cultural. For Tayo "the fifth world" of the Pueblos has "become entangled with European names" (68) and he comes to believe that "there would be no peace and the people would have no rest until the entanglements had been unwound to the source" (69).

This desire to return to the source contains obvious dangers of a nostalgic and reactionary recoding, but Betonie's and Silko's insistence that all fundamentalist activities be resisted seems to offer a guard against this kind of attitude. I am of the opinion that *Ceremony* as a novel traces a precarious trajectory between a genuinely inventive local resistance and a deeply nostalgic recodification. The witchery which functions as Silko's diabolic myth for historical disruption and colonial violence, is a story told by a magician- witch, a story that becomes reality as it is being told. At the start of *Ceremony* Silko suggests that she herself is re-telling grand mother Spider's story and that this story, in fact, constitutes the novel as a whole, "I'm telling you the story she is thinking" (1). One aspect of what I call the contest of stories in *Ceremony* is the attempt by Silko to manage and to contain the malign power of the witchery story within the larger narrative of Grandmother Spider's story. As Tayo realizes at the end, the real contest is for the ending of the story and he must keep the story out of the reach of the destroyers if the ceremony is to be completed successfully. Throughout *Ceremony* the inner dynamics of this contest of narratives is presented as a conflict between competing economies, a conflict between an economy of reciprocity and small communities represented by gift exchange on the one hand, and on the other, a sacrificial economy gone wild under the impact of the contemporary political economy of internal colonization.

I have analyzed in the context of the novels of Bernard Malamud that the Jewish community is segregated in the American Society on the basis of religion. Further, the discussion on the novels of Richard Wright also reveals the racial discrimination of Afro-Americans on color line. And both these communities are not usually accepted by the dominant European American Community. On the other hand, the Native-Americans on their own do not like to conform to the values of the dominant society. Moreover, they are marginalized in the American society because of their relative primitiveness.

The story of Kaup'a'ta, the gambler, one of the many smaller narratives that makes up the larger narrative of drought and witchery in *Ceremony* dramatizes these two economies in conflict. kaup'a'ta is a ck'o'yo magician who tricks people into gambling with him and gains power over his duped victims by feeding them blue cornmeal into which he has mixed human blood. All the victims eventually gamble away their lives and are themselves sacrificed to make the blue cornmeal mixture that will overpower other victims "He hung them upside down in his storeroom, Side by side with other victims. He cut out their hearts and let their blood run down into the bins of blue cornmeal" (172).

When Kaup'a'ta captures the storm clouds, thus causing a drought, the Sun, their father, takes gifts of blue and yellow pollen, tobacco and coral beads to grandmother Spider in order to find a way of freeing the clouds.

The Spiderwoman advises him about the most useful strategy to use against Kaup'a'ta and the sun succeeds in his mission. Gambling and the violence of witchery are, then, opposed to gift relationships and Silko directly links the freeing of the rain clouds with the curative ceremony undertaken by Tayo. As an act of triumph the sun does not kill Kaup'a'ta but cuts out his eyes and throws them into the sky where they become "the horizon stars of autumn" (176). Immediately after this Tayo, in "late September" (178) sees the stars drawn by Betonie to mark the final stage of his curative ceremony. What most distinguishes Silko's myth of malign magic is her transformation of local oral narratives into a comprehensive cosmological mapping of evil. Such a globalization, familiar in Christianity is, in fact, not found in the Native-American cultures of the South west. Although there is some belief in witchcraft at Laguna and in other Pueblo cultures, Silko has explained that the primary source of materials for her narrative of the witchery was the numerous stories of witchery and malign magic, she heard on the Navojo reservation at Chinle, Arizona, where belief in witchcraft is much more widespread and much more a part of everyday life than at Laguna. But while Silko has drawn upon these stories in *Ceremony,* the largest part of the witchery myth in the novel, the narrative of witchery's creation of White people and its manipulation of Whites as the primary instruments of a horrific and global destruction, is almost entirely Silko's own creation.

The transformation of witchcraft in both Silko's *Ceremony* and in Navajo culture can be viewed as responses to contact with White political and economic institutions and controls. *Ceremony* offers a dramatization of sacrificial narratives, that is, for want of a better way of putting it, more self-consciously critical than the folk practices of either the Navajo or the Quechua. Throughout *Ceremony* narratives of gift exchange are juxtaposed to the sacrificial narratives. In a story of the drought dissociated from the witchery stories, corn woman, angered by her sister Reed woman, leaves this world and retires to the fourth world below. In order to bring her back Fly and Hummingbird have to take her gifts of pollen, turquoise beads, and prayer sticks: "They gave her blue pollen and yellow pollen they gave her turquoise beads they gave her prayer sticks" (105). They also have to give similar gifts to Buzzard so that he will purify the town before corn woman returns. These stories reveal the reciprocal relationship between the human world and Nature. Tayo is witness to the ritual enactment of such reciprocity in his childhood. He remembers that when as a young boy he went deer hunting with his uncles Josiah and Robert and his cousin Rocky, his uncles sprinkled pinches of cornmeal on the dead deer's nose in order to feed "the deer's spirit": "They had to show their love and respect, their appreciation; otherwise, the deer would be offended, and they would not come to die for them the following year" (51). This attitude stands in stark contrast to that of the white loggers who shoot bears and mountain lions around the Pueblo region "for sport" (186). Silko, at this stage points out the difference in the attitude between the Native-Americans and the White Americans as to their attachment with the land and animals. In the very last stage of his ceremonial healing, when he is searching for his uncle's lost cattle, Tayo remembers the necessity for such a reciprocal offering and sprinkles pollen onto the tracks of a mountain lion, "the hunter's helper" (196) in Pueblo mythology. It is the mountain lion, who then saves Tayo's life by leading the White armed patrolmen away from him. Josiah, Robert and Tayo, all nourish the spirit of the gift, what the Maori call the "hau". The pollen is a return gift that ensures that the circle of reciprocity is not broken. In the words of Lewis Hyde, "nature's abundance is in fact a consequence of man's treating its wealth as a gift" (*The Gift* 19).

Just as the violence of Emo and the others against Harley shifts the oral witchery narrative, presented throughout in verse form, into the main prose narrative of the novel, so the lesson of reciprocity taught by the oral gift narratives finds its fullest embodiment in the dramatization of the second half of Tayo's ceremonial healing. This second half, beginning after Tayo leaves Betonie's hut, dominates the last part of the novel Tayo sets out on a quest to find his uncle's lost cattle, encounters and sleeps with the women Ts'eh Montano, relearns those structures of attention that place him in a balanced relationship with the land, and completes his cure by retrieving the cattle from the White ranchers and returning to Laguna. By the end of the novel it is the stories of gift and reciprocity that seem to triumph. Silko seems to have celebrated the ultimate victory of Native American culture and in the novel she attempts to materialize this objective as in *The Assistant*, Malamud celebrates the ultimate triumph of Judaism after Frank Alpine becomes a Jew. It is not blood sacrifice that regenerates the land. The hero is cured and the rains come before the crucifixion of Harley. Tayo is tempted to intervene in the final scene of "sparagmos" to save Harley by killing Emo, but stops himself from doing so, believing that to meet violence with violence would be to abandon himself to the logic of the witchery. And while the scene in the uranium mine is the climactic moment of the novel, it is not the last. It is followed by the conclusion of the oral gift narrative where Corn Mother accepts the gifts brought to her by Hummingbird and Fly and returns to the human world: "We finally got it but it sure wasn't very easy. 'Okay', Buzzard said 'Go back and tell them I'll purify the town'.... The storm clouds returned the grass and plants started growing again" (255-56).

Silko's attempt to maintain a double resolution in her novel, not to make regeneration dependent upon sacrifice, appears at first as a resistance to the most common and pernicious form of the sacrificial-regenerative narrative patterns found in Western cultures. What is problematic about Silko's apparent resistance to such a globalization of sacrificial mythology is the overarching plot-form of her own novel: from the dislocations of the "wounded" hero in a drought ridden land to the inevitable climax of sacrifice, regeneration, and healing. Despite the apparent dissociation of the two economies in *Ceremony*, the resolutions of both narratives do form a united or synchronized climax to the book where the sacrificial working-out of the witchery is placed as an integral part of the ongoing ceremony outlined by Betonie for Tayo. It is in this sense that the disconnection engineered by Silko is overridden by the utter predictability and inevitability of her instantly recognizable plot structure. *Ceremony* as a novel remains a structure of contradictions, that in its most interesting moments, energizes itself by dramatizing these very contradictions, but at its weakest points unravels its precarious local critical practice into a historical nostalgia for mythical transcendence. Silko has been successful in presenting her viewpoint as to preserving the Native-American ethnic values in an atmosphere surrounded by the hostile European Americans. Like Richard Wright, Leslie Marmon Silko also shows her concern for her community of people and their welfare in her novels. In the preceding chapter I have shown how Wright was always preoccupied with the problems of the Afro-Americans and he used his writings as a platform to ventilate their grievances. Towards the end of *Ceremony* Silko is seen as a custodian of the ethnicity of her community and she is not at all influenced or affected by the dominant society. Her voice against the White Americans persists throughout the novel and she asserts that theirs is a culture, which is by no means inferior or subordinate to the Anglo culture. Her voice of accusation and resistance which characterizes the novel *Ceremony* finds a literary transmission in her second novel *Almanac of the Dead* which came out in the year 1991. In fact, *Ceremony* established her reputation as an important writer and won her a five year Mac Arthur Foundation "genius" grant in 1981. This grant helped her start work on the *Almanac of the Dead.*

With seventy characters and a wide spectrum of events spanning 500 years and several continents, the plot of *Almanac of the Dead* is less a linear than an elaborate web of events. Peopled with addicts, alcoholics, corrupt judges and politicians, unscrupulous and greedy land speculators, and a host of other unsavory characters, the novel also tells the story of resistance to Euro-American oppression and a growing effort of indigenous people and their allies to retake the land and ultimately to become agents of its healing. The basic themes of the novel have been the folk stories of the past, pronouncements on the present and predictions of a dire future for the offspring of the European conquerors. *Almanac of the Dead* is a touching account of events set against a backdrop of sweeping historical and geopolitical forces and changes. This has been a very popular novel as most of the events of the novel take place in Tucson where Silko resides. The novel deals with issues like environmental destruction, water scarcity, sprawl, war profiteering, the homeless, indigenous land rights, racism, the border disputes, corruption, colonialism and the spiritual bankruptcy of Western culture. The novel contains a variety of characters, plot threads, and places. Some of the threads intersect directly, some only refer to each other, and some never come together, or are just the historical background. In the novel we come across Lecha and Zeta, two Yaqui Indian twin sisters who live on the outskirts of Tucson. In her youth Lecha was given by her grandmother a bundle of ancient notebooks called *The Almanac of the Dead* that have been handed down through many generations of indigenous people in Mexico. The almanac tells the story of these people, who fled from the south of Mexico, centuries ago to escape "the destroyers" (18), sorcerers who practised blood sacrifice and became the Aztec rulers. The Almanac is also a history of the arrival of the Europeans in the new world and a prophecy foretelling their departure from it.

Lecha hires another main character Seese, a "Coke addict from San Diego" (26), to help her transcribe the Almanac into a computer, because Lecha is getting old. Seese has come to Tucson to find Lecha, because Lecha has psychic powers that allow her to find murder victims, and Seese wants to find out if her kidnapped baby has died. Meanwhile, Zeta and Farro, Lecha's son, have become drug smugglers along with some other local Yaquis.

Down in Chiapas, another Subplot involves a corrupt general and his business partner who are getting guns form the U.S.A. They are worried about a recent upsurge of indigenous restlessness in the region. La Escapia is a Mayan woman who is part of a secret army of poor villagers all over Chiapas preparing for an armed rebellion, "remember, this was written at least three years before the Zapatista uprising!" (129). She goes to Mexico city to attend a secret Cuban "Freedom School" (138) that teaches about Marxism in exchange for providing arms and weapons for insurgents around Latin America. The Mayans don't care about Cuba or Marx, but their main intention is to get weapons to take back their land. This idea is an act of reinforcement of the idea present in *Ceremony*. Meanwhile, back in Tucson an East Coast Mafia family is starting to move in on Zeta's smuggling operation. They work with a corrupt senator and a clandestine agent from the CIA to smuggle arms into southern Mexico and Central America in exchange for cocaine. They're also involved in real estate development and building huge water-sucking suburbs, buying off judges to head off the environmental lawsuits filed against them. A person is also seen involved in a "biomaterial" business that secretly harvests organs and plasma from homeless people and Indians.

Another incident that emerges in the course of development of the plot is, Seese's ex-boyfriend, an artist named David, who is with some rich racist drug dealers from Argentina and Columbia named Beaufrey and Serlo. David kidnaps his and Seese's baby and heads down to Serlo's ranch in Columbia with Beaufrey, but Beaufrey gets jealous and has the baby kidnapped from David and makes it look like Seese did it. During all this Serlo is working on a crazy post apocalypse eugenics scheme to preserve the "sangre pura" (237) master race in sealed biospheres at his ranch.

A close look at these events described in the text shows how complex the web that Silko weaves is. It's really addictive reading, infused with a dark ambiance, great historical anecdotes and references to the injustices of the past, as well as tons of moral ambiguity. Virtually every major character, with a few exceptions, is a corrupt person. The narrative revolves round the western hemisphere and over the last 500 years. In the novel, Tucson in the state of Arizona functions as a focal point, with much of the action radiating away from or towards the city. Arizona is experiencing the effects of a declining economy and devastating drought and growing civil unrest in Mexico. The narrator reminds the readers of the prophecy, the inexorable movement of the people in north, and while it may take 500 or 5000 years, the indigenous and their allies will reclaim the diseased and corrupted land. The theme of resistance to the Western forces works in the novel and Silko inserts a host of characters who work as part of this resistance movement. Among them are the twin sisters Lecha and Zeta; the twin brothers Tacho and EI Feo. Both brothers commune with the spirit macaws for advice. There is an "army of the Homeless" (86) who plan to retake "stolen" goods and land from the wealthy. The Barefoot Hopi Organizes incarcerated prisoners for an uprising against the U.S.government. Many of these and other characters converge at the novel's end at the International Holistic Healer's convention where "German root doctors" and "Celtic leech handlers" join hands with "new-age spiritualists" and the Green vengeance eco-warriors.

The malaise the novel describes is overwhelming. Most horrible are the forces of evil and the nightmare of the contemporary social contract in America. Those who can afford to have gone mad with technological idolatry and material gain. This creates an atmosphere of widespread disregard for all human lives, unless it directly serves the interests of the wealthy. In this setting *Almanac of the Dead* brings several medical issues to the foreground. One character, Trigg, owns a profitable blood plasma business and adds to his growing income through the illegal trade in human organs, using the body parts of street people and other "human debris", as he calls them. Trigg also plans to build a mega medical complex in Tucson for monetary gain.

In Silko's texts, legends and stories of the past and the future are interwoven in the contemporaneity of the present moment. In *Almanac,* the key fragment that Lecha must use to decipher the old almanac describes the sacred moment as the present moment. The Pueblo Indian oral tradition that informs Silko's texts encodes the cultural experience of her people. The oral narrative, or story, becomes the medium through which the Pueblo knowledge and belief was maintained. Old stories are kept alive by adapting to the changing context of the people's lives. Oral story telling operates at two levels— at one level it is the representation of an incident that had happened a long time ago and at another level it is the actual enactment of the incident itself.

The storytelling that Calabazas in *Almanac* remembers, involves everybody. Thus, everybody "one by one,... contributed some detail or opinion or alternative version. The story they told did not run in a line for the horizon but circled and spiraled instead like the red tailed hawk" (224). Silko herself assumes the role of a tribal story teller who in writing her *Almanac* wants the reader to listen to her stories. In mapping out the topological terrain of Native-American experience, her work operates at the level of dreams for a better society for her people. The experience of Silko's *Almanac* does not lie in any single narrative thread but somewhere within the web of different threads in the relationship they forge with one another. Tacho, one of the twin brothers leading the poor people's Army towards north, wants to fight his wars at the level of dreams whereas Lecha fights her war at the level of words by decoding the old almanac and making it accessible to people. Similarly, Silko by writing her revolutionary *Almanac* engages in a war that is fought at the level of stories because she herself points out that for her the only way to seek justice is through the power of the stories.

Silko's *Ceremony* seems to single out capitalistic modes of operation as one of the major factors responsible for the continued oppression of people as well as the desecration of the earth. The novel proposes that the oppressed people, especially the indigenous people of America, can forge alliances across the borders and fight the White hegemony that the text associates with the capitalistic modes of production. The Native-Americans who live in this world of corruption and decadence cannot completely keep themselves free from the violent lifestyle of their oppressors, also referred to as "the destroyers" in Silko's writings. In such a world of violence, Lecha's remembering of the forgotten cultural history becomes an act of deliverance of life in the barren terrain where death mimics as life. As the transcriber and decoder of the old almanac, Lecha becomes the guardian of collective memory and tribal history, thereby becoming the tribe's story teller. The analysis of *Ceremony* and *Almanac* reveals the successful literary rendition of the mission of Leslie Silko. Her voice of resistance and antagonism towards the dominant society is evident in both the texts. Silko assumes an important role in preserving and perpetuating the Native-American cultural ethos. She believes in the sanctity and power of Native-American "stories" which can really sustain them in future as it is visible in the opening pages of *Ceremony:* "I will tell you something about stories. They aren't just entertainment. Don't be fooled. They are all we have, you see, all we have to fight off illness and death" (2). The same tone of resistance is also found in the works of N. Scott Momaday, another prominent Native-American novelist belonging to Kiowa tribe. Momaday also celebrates the richness of his Native-American heritage. His *House Made of Dawn,* an epoch-making novel celebrates the natural richness of American Southwest. In telling the story of Abel, a young Indian, in need of healing and restoration of spirit, Momaday showed the significance of Indian religious traditions and the role these traditions play in Abel's healing from war, from contempt, from racism, and from the United States government's policy of social engineering. At the same time, virtually every page introduces the reader to the integration of religious forms into the everyday life of the Pueblo people. The major part of the book is an expression of Momaday's love for growing up Indian in the Southwest. Both Silko and Momaday appear to be the custodians of Native-American culture. Silko's writings aim at arousing an ethnic consciousness among the people of her community. Silko's novels demonstrate her sense of commitment and belongingness to the Native-American values and literature. Both these novels of Silko glorify the Native-American ethnicity and offer a very meaningful insight into the very experience of what it has meant to be a Native-American in modern times.

5

Conclusion

In the three preceding chapters covering Jewish-American, Afro-American, and Native-American novels, I have tried to show different facets of the American ethnic literature. American ethnic literature continues to be more and more "ethnic" because the writers coming under this category continue to be inspired by their respective ethnic roots and values. Such a tendency on the part of the ethnic writers cannot be called "Un-American" because the uniqueness of American literature lies in its diversity in terms of ethnicity. Right from the beginning of the European-American civilization in the early seventeenth century, people from different parts of the globe have immigrated to America in search of opportunities. So, it is obvious that the quest for opportunities has been common to all the ethnic groups. Different ethnic groups have tried to materialize this aspiration in different ways. However, since the Americans of European origin outnumbered other ethnic communities like the Native-Americans and the Afro-Americans, they have tried to exert some amount of control over others which gave rise to ethnic confrontations. This idea of ethnic confrontation is clearly discernible in the works of Malamud, Wright and Silko. The natural outcome of this confrontation is "suffering" for the minority communities at the hands of the dominant European-American community. Malamud has analyzed this theme of suffering born out of confrontation in his novels from a Jewish perspective. But at the same time, he advocates for a life of values, order and dignity for his fellow Jews. For him, feeling for human suffering is far from being an exclusively "Jewish" quality, although he is at times inclined to speak of suffering as the mark of the Jew alone and as his very fate. Frank Alpine in *The Assistant,* thinking of what it means to be a Jew, explains it to himself thus: "That's what they live for... to suffer. And the one who has got the biggest pain in the gut and can hold onto it longest without running to the toilet is the best Jew. No wonder they got on his nerves (*The Assistant* 74). This is, of course, an outsider's point of view, and it remains for Morris Bober, the unlucky and impoverished owner of the grocery store, to correct his Italian Assistant's assertion that Jews like to suffer because : "if you live, you suffer, some people suffer more, but not because they want. But I think if a Jew don't suffer for the law, he will suffer for nothing" (*The Assistant* 106). Malamud tries to transcend all kinds of sectarian understanding of suffering by looking at it as the fate of the whole of mankind, which can only be mitigated when all men assume responsibility for each other. The contrast between the Jew and the Gentile can thus be resolved on the level of feeling and a society based upon the Dostoevskyan idea of Universal brotherhood and mutual responsibility can be established.

Malamud does not praise the existence of suffering

or say that human beings should seek it out. But his view is that since it is bound to be there as a part of human life, it should be used as an aid to moral growth. Malamud frequently uses the figure of the schlemiel, a victim with a comic aspect, to depict the human condition in modern times. This figure brings forth compassion rather than mockery and ridicule; pathos is the primary emotion elicited as the schlemiel's situation moves close to tragedy. Malamud, in all the three novels that I have analyzed, has explored the various levels of Jewish consciousness of his characters. Morris Bober, Yakov Bok and Harry Lesser are three Jewish characters standing for three facets of the Jewish ethnicity. Morris Bober follows the tradition of the heroes of Yiddish folktales who mutter to themselves and complain loudly, with ironic self-deprecation, about the difficulties of their lot in life. His neighbor Karp, the owner of the well-stocked liquor store fears a robbery, but ultimately Morris is robbed. Fully aware of the absurdity of his impoverished store being the target of burglars, while Karp's "pleasure palace" stands untouched next door, Morris thinks to himself: "The end fitted the day. It was his luck, others had better" (*The Assistant* 22). Throughout the novel, like the traditional hard-luck characters of Yiddish folklore, Morris is the unwitting architect of his own misfortune. In this respect Morris Bober stands for the ethical facet of Jewish ethnicity.

Yakov Bok, the Jewish character in *The Fixer* adds another dimension to Jewish ethnicity as his is a different predicament. He is fully aware of the problem of being a Jew in a foreign land and tries to hide his Jewish identity but finally he had to pay a heavy price for his act of concealing the Jewish identity. His intention was to better his life in Russia but that did not work out. Yakov is seen rebelling against the Tsarist regime. He has adopted a violent tone to establish his innocence in a corrupt place like the Tsarist Russia and like Morris Bober, he also suffers, but his suffering has an existential overtone. I would like to say that Yakov's plight represents the existential facet of Jewish ethnicity.

The Tenants offers a very pessimistic picture of American ethnicity. Malamud has linked life to art in this novel and highlights the fact that ethnicity as a social force operates at the psychic level of the writers as well. I have observed in *The Tenants* that no writer can be alienated from his ethnic background. Both Harry and Willie struggle as writers to put into order on paper, elements of their experiences. Each writer becomes the other's victim because neither is capable of a sufficient depth of sympathy for the struggles and limitations of the other. Their prejudices and lack of understanding lead to mutual destruction. This animosity between them had its impact on their craft as well: "whereas Willie tries to create art out of life, Lesser tries to discover life through his art. Neither is successful" (Mesher 62). Willie dislikes Harry's insistence on form because he sees it as the White man's way. Unfortunately, Willie cannot see literature without the avoidance of form as opposed to the "White" order and the mind. Above all, Willie wants power for his people and for himself, and he hopes to create action through his words. His pseudonym, Bill Spear, combines overtones of literature and violence in contrast to Harry Lesser's name, which exudes self-control and passionlessness. Through his new name, Willie wishes to obliterate his past and become a new person. As David Mesher observes that "Willie, in many ways, is a 'nigger': the stereotyped ghetto black. Bill, the devoted artist, is not.... Willie, unable to be Bill, reverts to the stereotype of the ghetto black..." (67). Malamud tends to suggest that if the interracial relationship in the American society does not improve, it is bound to have an adverse impact on ethnic literature as well. In the light of the novel *The Tenants* I would say that Harry Lesser stands for the creative facet of Jewish ethnicity.

In all the three novels of Malamud, I have tried to show the growing dissatisfaction of the protagonists towards the White society. In Richard Wright's *Native Son* and *Black Boy* the same sort of dissatisfaction is evident. In *Native Son* personal bitter experiences of Wright are reflected. Bigger Thomas, a Southern black relocated in Chicago's Ghetto, finds himself trapped in the dilemma imposed upon him by the White society. He desperately dreams of full humanity but ironically begins to achieve it only in violence that brings about his own destruction and that of two White women. He stands as the supreme symbol of America's angry black men. Wright's *Black Boy* remains the best account of what it meant to grow up black in Mississippi. Wright seems to have left out little in the novel: the black child's hunger, fear, and loneliness, his vulnerability to the contempt of Whites and the harsh discipline imposed by his black elders, presumably to prepare him for life in a world where blacks were expected to know their place, his repeated exploitation by black and White alike and his perpetual humiliation. *Native Son* as a black novel is comparable with Ellison's *Invisible Man*. Both reflect in realistic detail, circumstances that their respective authors encountered while growing up black in a segregated South. Bigger Thomas, like Wright himself has grown up in Mississippi, where the shadow of slavery has persisted, and the traumas forced upon him in youth have rendered him permanently angry at being denied the dignity that he instinctively knows is rightfully his. By contrast, the nameless hero of *Invisible Man* is repeatedly advised by the Whites and the Blacks alike that his place in the society is somewhat lower than that of his White counterparts. The reason of Bigger's being so hostile and self-assertive is obvious. The episode with the rat seems less a symbol than a catalyst for feelings of helplessness and worthlessness that Bigger has carried unexpressed for some time. It is a sort of uprising against such feelings that causes him to disappoint his mother and distress his sister: "Vera went behind the curtain and Bigger heard her trying to comfort his mother. He shut their voices out of his mind. He hated his family because he knew that they were suffering and that he was powerless to help them...he would be swept out of himself with fear and despair" (*Native Son* 14). It is striking that Bigger who suspends all reactions in order to keep away from killing goes into a deep physiological resolution of not to react to anything. Killing does not release feeling in any basic way, but merely rebounds into not feeling, into not daring to feel. When Bigger identifies himself with the act of killing, we need to take a close account of two facts: to acknowledge the killing is to go past the mere act and the ensuing "physiological resolution not to react" into a stage of open awareness and responsibility; and to accept this stage is to defeat the numbing depression that kept him from himself, his family and his society, and thus it entails the beginning of his active humanity. It is his ability to face the killing, not merely to perform it, that counts most in the end. The performance is in itself a reflex of the self-cancellation that marks Bigger at the outset.

Wright recounts one incident with his mother on her deathbed. He writes, "Once, in the night, my mother called me to her bed and told me that she could not endure the pain that she wanted to die. I held her hand and begged her to be quiet. That night I ceased to react to my mother, my feelings were frozen" (*Black Boy* 111). Wright, in the emotional realm matches his mother's position in the physical: he cannot endure the pain. His mother dies, according to the dictates of nature. Seeing the same reaction in Bigger, gives us important evidence of his sensitivity and makes plausible his eventual emergence, or rebirth from self protection that causes him to kill Mary Dalton and Bessie as he has earlier metaphorically killed himself.

The purpose of *Native Son* is to assert the point of view of Wright as to the relationship of the Negroes with the American society. The "native son" in his eyes, could only be the Black American. Bigger Thomas' culture is the history of the Black American and it coincides precisely with the founding and duration of the United States. From 1619 to the modern times, Black American culture has grown and flourished. Wright had a vision of his own. He had certainly envisioned a better America, an America free from racism. The Negroes of his time might not have experienced that phase of history, but the kind of foundation stone he had laid with the help of his writings is definitely giving rich dividends in present day times. Afro-Americans in the present day society are enjoying a place, which was denied to their forefathers years ago. The White American society has changed a lot in terms of its attitude towards the Negroes. Afro-Americans in modern times are occupying very vital positions in different spheres of American administration. The color of the negroes is no more considered to be a stigma, on the other hand, it adds to the color of the American society and ethnicity.

As I have pointed out in the contexts of Bernard Malamud, and Richard Wright that they feel the necessity of voicing the feelings of their community in order to preserve and protect their respective ethnic traditions, the same is true of Leslie Marmon Silko whose primary mission of writing is to glorify the richness of Native-American heritage. In both *Ceremony* and *Almanac of the Dead,* Silko, who was born and raised on the Laguna reservation in New Mexico, does not only condemn the White European descendants who invaded her people's country, but also openly confronts the problems of her own people. Just as she portrays the European-Americans as unmerciful invaders, she also portrays Native-Americans as forgotten citizens left in the dark to become cultural misfits caught in a precipitous downward spiral that has led them to severe problems such as alcoholism, crime, and intransigence. They are a people who have sacrificed their spiritual awareness for spiritless worlds of poverty and moral ambiguity. But it is not their fault, she complains. It is what they have been left with. In *Almanac,* actions take place in literal as well as metaphorical borderlands, which separate the U.S from Mexico. Silko's borderlands represent a world of people of heterogeneous histories who came together occupying the fringes of psychological, emotional and social landscape. They are engaged in different discourses, threads of which run across the borderline, extending deep into the regions of Mexico, over into the edges of Central America. The common thread of these discourses is the capitalistic exploitation of the people, the stories of those who are being exploited and those who do the exploiting. In *Almanac,* this is testified by Rambo's Homeless Army on one side of the border and El Feo's Army of the poor people on the other side of the U.S-Mexico border. The members of both armies are outside the cycle of both the production as well as consumption. Silko is always opposed to the idea of modernizing the Native-American people as the process of modernization may make their culture extinct. Silko is proud of her rich cultural heritage and she wants to transmit the various facets of her ethnicity to posterity. As La Vonne Ruoff has argued:

"Silko emphasizes the need to return to the rituals and oral traditions of the past in order to rediscover the basis for one's cultural identity. Only when this is done is one prepared to deal with the problems of the present...Silko demonstrates that the Keres rituals and traditions have survived all attempts to eradicate them and that the seeds for the resurgence of their power lie in the memories and creativeness of her people" (15).

In *Ceremony* when Tayo resists all the forces that have been turned against Pueblo holiness, he acts like the legendary Arrowboy. Although Tayo had been taught in school to scorn the old stories, he believes in them and understands their modernity, their applicability to his situation. Silko also makes fun of the White people and their way of life. The White people thought that protestant Christianity should replace Laguna paganism even though as a token of appreciation for Indian culture they sometimes express a surprising certitude that, "this once great culture is being lost or replaced by an Anglo culture that does not have the same respect for nature... and is in some ways morally inferior to it" (Blicksilver158). The intensity of feeling for her culture as reflected in her novels affirms that Indian culture still exists and has the potential to transform the Anglo-culture. As she said in an interview in 1978, "These things will only die if we neglect to tell the stories. So I am telling the stories" (Seyersted, "Two" 28). Silko also highlights the vices that are associated with the White people. One such example is the drunkenness that destroys the Native-American identity. *Ceremony* presents alcohol as something destructive of, or inconsistent with Indian traditions and identity. It is only after Tayo rejects alcoholism, he is shown thriving and living in harmony with his family and with the land, while his erstwhile friends slaughter one another in orgies of drunken violence. We see Tayo, fully recovered at the end of *Ceremony.* Silko meticulously portrays the ultimate triumph of the "traditional" over the "modern" in *Ceremony,* where Tayo's cure involves the traditional arts of sand painting and singing, both of which are necessary elements in the Navajo curative ritual administered by Betonie. As the Indian tradition is embodied largely in songs in *Ceremony,* the act of singing is set up in implicit opposition to everything that conflicts with that tradition: the passivity of reservation life, increasing secularism, White exploitation and alcoholism. This kind concern of Silko for her own people makes her one of the foremost Native-American novelists. Silko does not hesitate to blame the Europeans for their hundreds of years of crimes. She is of the opinion that while there are several tribes, there is only one world.

The novels of Bernard Malamud, Richard Wright and Leslie Marmon Silko strongly affirm the ethnic elements in American literature. These ethnic elements also constitute a significant aspect of American culture. The diverse nature of American culture is usually reflected in the American literature, which comes under the category of American ethnic literature. In 1963 Nathan Glazer and Daniel Patrick Moynihan based their provocative analysis of New York City's ethnic dynamism in their book *Beyond the Melting pot* on the belief that "the powerful assimilatory influences of American society operate on all who come into it". They thought that America's ethnic groups were peoples who had been recreated as something new. The publication of *Beyond the Melting pot* also paved the way for the revival of American ethnic identification in the 1960s and 1970s when attacks on the melting pot became the battle cry of "Unmeltable ethnics" who admonished their followers to pay attention to ethnicity and to give up the assimilationist hope that ethnicity was going to disappear. Yet, given the nature of American society it could not or did not assimilate the immigrant groups fully or in equal degree.

Assimilation is, however, a two-way process. It is rarely accomplished rapidly, because in the socialization of ethnic group members, aspects of the group's culture, values, norms, even behavioral and identificational patterns are transmitted across generations. It is contingent upon the willingness of the dominant society to accept persons who had been in particular ethnic communities. Moreover, both must wish to disregard the old boundaries. Assimilation is thus the culmination of multistage, multi-dimensional, overlapping processes, simultaneously occurring among people at different points in relation to the dominant society.

A multitude of ethnic communities have spanned the spectrum of relationships in America with each other and with the larger society. In this reality of American pluralism—as part of the two-way process—ethnic group members have adapted to and incorporated for themselves, various components of the dominant culture's values, norms, behavioral and associational patterns, and mainstream identification. In doing so, they have integrated into that general society and have influenced many of its characteristics, too. At the same time, many continue with similarly varying degrees of intensity and commitment, to maintain their separateness—their boundaries—and to adhere to their traditional cultures, associations, networks, identities and historical memories. Many groups like the Natïve-Americans strive to preserve the elements of their ethnicity and ethnic identity and to transmit them to their children. The Native-Americans had no desire at all to assimilate, being content with their ethnicity. There were also some groups like the Afro-Americans who had all the desire for complete acceptance but had met with enduring barriers. American ethnicity has been a source of frustration for those, for whom their ethnicity has not been voluntary, who have largely been denied any choice and who have over the decades continued to rely upon their ethnic communities for coping with that reality.

Though American ethnicity involves several diverse elements, yet it adds to the strength of the nation and the American people in general who take pride in being what they are. It is the presence of ethnicity in American society, which elevates the place of the country to a "Super power". In fact, the ethnic nature of American literature adds to its literary fragrance. Whether they write in other languages or in English, ethnic writers have an acute sense of doubleness—"Double consciousness", an Emersonian term used in W.E. B.Dubois's well-known formula of "an American, a Negro" which exerted its pressure upon ethnic writers as cultural producers. Ethnic writers in general confront an actual or imagined double audience, composed of 'insiders" and of readers, listeners, or spectators who are not familiar with the writer's ethnic group. Here the opportunity presents itself for the writer to play a variety of roles. Imperceptibly and sometimes involuntarily, writers begin to function as translators of ethnicity to ignorant and sometimes hostile outsiders and at the same time, as mediators between America and greenhorns. A century after Whitman, it is useful to think of America as a polyethnic nation among polyethnic nations instead of the "nation of nations". While the diverse nature of the American society might pose some problems for the administration, it offers new avenues for the researchers of American ethnic literature.

Bibliography

Adamic, Louis. *From Many Lands.* New York: Harper, 1940.

Alter, Iska. *The Good Man's Dilemma: Social Criticism in the Fiction of Bernard Malamud.* New York: AMS Press, 1981.

Antin,Mary. *The Promised Land.* Boston: Houghton Mifflin, 1912.

Astro, Richard and Benson, Jackson J. eds. *The Fiction of Bernard Malamud.* Corvallis: Oregon State University Press, 1977.

Bakish, David. *Richard Wright.* New York: Frederick Unger, 1973.

Baldwin, James. *Notes of a Native Son.* Boston: Beacon Press, 1955.

Baraka, Amiri, and Neal, Larry, eds.Black *Fire: An Anthology of Afro-American Writing.* New York: Morrow, 1968.

Bellow, Saul. "Starting Out in Chicago", *The American Scholar* 44 (Winter1974-1975): 72.

Blicksilver, Edith. "Traditionalism vs. Modernity: Leslie Silko on American Indian Women". *Southwest Review* 64: 1979, 149-60.

Bloom, Harold.Ed.*Bernard Malamud*.New York: Chelsea House Publishers, 1986.

Bone, Robert. *The Negro Novel in America*. New Haven: Yale University Press, 1958.

Brignano, Carl Russell. *Richard Wright: An Introduction to the Man and his Works*. Pittsburgh: University of Pittsburgh Press, 1970.

Bryer, Jackson. "Richard Wright: A Selected Checklist of Criticism". *Wisconsin Studies in Contemporary Literature* 1(Fall 1960):22-23.

Buber, Martin. *I and Thou*. Edinburgh: T. and T. Clark, 1970.

Daiches, David. *Partisan Review* May - June (1940): 244 - 45.

Davidson, Basil. *The African Slave Trade*. Boston: Atlantic Monthly Press, 1961.

Debo,Angie. *A History of the Indians of the United States*. Norman: University of Oklahoma Press,1977.

Ducharme, Robert. *Art and Idea in the Novels of Bernard Malamud*. The Hague: Mouton, 1974.

Elizabeth N. Evasdaughter. "Leslie Marmon Silko's *Ceremony*: Healing Ethnic Hatred by Mixed-Breed Laughter". *MELUS* 15.1 (Spring 1988):83-95.

Ellison, Ralph. *Shadow and Act*. New York: Random House, 1964.

Emanuel, James and Gross, Theodore L.,eds. *Dark Symphony: Negro Literature in America*. New York: Free Press, 1960.

Fabian, Ilona. "The Transformation of Culture Knowledge and the Emergence of Ethnicity among Czech Immigrants in Chicago". Unpublished research proposal, Department of Anthropology, University of Chicago, 1972.

Fabre Michel. *The Unfinished Quest of Richard Wright.* New York: William Morrow & Co., 1973.

Fanon, Frantz. *Black Skins, White Masks.* New York: Evergreen Cat Book, 1967.

Feagin, Joe R. *Racial and Ethnic Relations.* New Jersey: Prentice Hall, 1978.

Fiedler, Leslie. "Negro and Jew: Encounter in America". *No! In Thunder: Essays on Myth and Literature.* London: Eyre and Spottiswoode, 1963:241.

Fiedler, Leslie. *To the Gentiles.* New York: Stein and Day, 1972.

Field, Leslie A., and Joyce W. Field, eds. *Bernard Malamud and the Critics.* New York: New York University Press, 1970.

Field, Leslie A., and Joyce W. Field, eds. *Bernard Malamud: A collection of critical essays* .New Jersey: Prentice Hall, 1975.

Frankel, Haskel. "Bernard Malamud". *Saturday Review* 10 September 1966:37-38.

Friedberg, Maurice. "History and Imagination: Two Views of the Beilis Case". *Midstream* 12.9(Nov.1966):72-76.

Friedman, Alan Warren. "Bernard Malamud: The Hero as Schnook". *Southern Review* 4.4(Oct.1968):927-944.

Girgus, Sam. *The New Covenant: Jewish Writers and the American Idea.* Chapel Hill: University of North Carolina Press, 1984.

Glazer, Nathan and Daniel P. Moynihan. *Beyond the Melting Pot.* Cambridge: MIT Press, 1970.

Gordon, Milton. *Assimilation in American Life.* New York: Oxford University Press, 1964.

Helterman,Jeffrey. *Understanding Bernard Malamud.* Columbia: University of South Carolina Press, 1985.

Hoilman, Dennis R. "'A World Made of Stories': An Interpretation of Leslie Silko's Ceremony". *South Dakota Review* 17.4(1979-80):54-66.

Hyde, Lewis. *Gift: Imagination and the Erotic Life of Property*. New York: Vintage Books, 1983.

Jahner, Elaine. "An Act of Attention: Event Structure in *Ceremony". American Indian Quarterly* 5.1(1979):37-46.

Josephy, Alvin M., Jr. *The Indian Heritage of America.* New York: Alfred A.Knopf, 1970.

Kallen, Horace M. *Cultural Pluralism and the American Idea* .Philadelphia: University of Pennsylvania Press, 1956.

Lincoln, Kenneth. *Native American Renaissance.* Berkley: University of California Press, 1983.

Malamud, Bernard. *God's Grace*. New York: Farrar, Straus and Giroux, 1982.

–. *The Assistant*. New Delhi: Oxford University Press, 1981.

—-. *The Fixer*. New York: Farrar, Straus and Giroux, 1966.

—-. *The Natural*. New York: Harcourt, Brace, 1952.

—-. *The Tenants*. New York: Farrar, Straus and Giroux, 1971.

Malin, Irving. *Jews and Americans*. Carbondale: Southern Illinois University Press, 1965.

Marriot, Alice and Carol K. Rachlin. *American Epic:The Story of the American Indian*. New York: Thomas Crowell, 1969.

Mays, Benjamin E. *The Image of God in Negro Literature*. New York: Russell and Russell,1938.

McCall, Dan.*The Example of Richard Wright*. New York: Harcourt, Brace &World, 1969.

Mesher, David R. "Names and Stereotypes in Malamud's '*The Tenants*' ". *Studies in American Jewish Literature* 4 (Spring 1978):62.

Mitchell, Carol. "Ceremony as Ritual". *American Indian Quarterly* 5.1(1979):27-35.

Momaday, N. Scott. *House Made of Dawn*. New York: Harper and Row, 1968.

Nicholas O. Warner. "Images of Drinking in 'Woman Singing', *Ceremony*, and *House Made of Dawn*". *MELUS* II. 4 (WINTER 1984):15-30.

Oswalt, Wendell H. *This Land Was Theirs: A study of the North American Indian*. New York: John Wiley,1966.

Ozick, Cynthia "Literary Blacks and Jews".*Midstream* 18 (1972):10-24.

Pinsker, Sanford. "The Achievement of Bernard Malamud". *Midwest Quarterly* 10 (summer 1969):379-89.

Pinsker, Sanford. *The Schlemiel as Metaphor*. Carbondale: Southern Illinois University Press, 1971.

Ray, David and Farnsworth, Robert. *Richard Wright: Impressions and Perspectives*.Ann Arbor: University of Michigan Press, 1973.

Richman, Sidney. Bernard Malamud. New York: Twayne, 1966.

Roth, Philip. "Writing About Jews", *Reading Myself and Others*. New York, 1975, 169.

Roth, Phillip. "The New Jewish Stereotypes". *American Judaism* 11 (winter 1961):49-51.

Rovit, Earl H. "Bernard Malamud and the Jewish Literary Tradition". *Critique* 3(Winter-spring 1960):3-10.

Ruoff, A. La Vonne. "Ritual and Renewal: Keres Traditions in the Short Fiction of Leslie Silko". *MELUS* 5.4 (1977): 2-17.

Russell, Howard S. *Indian New England before the Mayflower.* Hanover, N.H.: University press of New England, 1980.

Salzberg, Joel. *Bernard Malamud: A Reference Guide.* Boston: G.K. Hall & Co., 1985.

Schermerhorn, Richard A. *Comparative Ethnic Relations: A Framework For Theory and Research.* New York: Random House, 1969.

Scott, Nathan A., Jr. "Search for Beliefs: The Fiction of Richard Wright". University of Kansas City Review 23 (1956):19-24.

Scruggs, Charles. "'All Dressed Up But No Place to Go':The Black Writer and His Audience During the Harlem Renaissance". *American Literature* XLVIII, iv (January 1977): 543-563.

Seyersted, Per. "Two Interviews with Leslie Marmon Silko". *American Studies In Scandinavia* 13(1981): 17-33.

Shear,Walter. "Culture conflict in *The Assistant*". *Midwest Quarterly* 7 (Summer 1966):367-380.

Shenker,Israel. "For Malamud It's Story". *New York Times Book Review* 3 October 1971:22.

Silko, Leslie Marmon. *Almanac of the Dead.* New York: Simon and Schuster, 1991.

–. *Ceremony.* New York: Penguin, 1986.

–. *STORYTELLER.* New York: Arcade Publishing, 1981.

Skerrett, Joseph T. "The Wright Interpretation: Ralph Ellison and The Anxiety of Influence". *The Massachusetts Review* XXI, 1 (Spring 1980):196-212.

Stepto, Robert B. "Richard Wright and the Afro-American Literary Tradition". *The Massachusetts Review* XVIII, 3(Autumn 1977):525-541.

Stern, Daniel. "The Art of Fiction: Bernard Malamud". *Paris Review* 16 (spring - 1975): 40-64.

Tyler, Hamilton A. *Pueblo Gods and Myths.* Norman: University of Oklahoma Press, 1964.

W.E.B. Dubois. *The Souls of Black Folk: Three Negro Classics.* Ed. John Hope Franklin. New York: Avon, 1969.

Washington, Joseph. *Black Religion: The Negro and Christianity in the United States.* Boston : Beacon Press, 1966.

Webb, Constance. *Richard Wright: A Biography.* New York: G.P. Putnam's Sons, 1968.

Weisbord , Robert and Stein, Arthur.*Bittersweet Encounter: The Afro- American and the American Jew.* Connecticut: Negro Universities Press, 1970.

Weisbord, Robert and Stein, Arthur. *Bittersweet Encounter: The Afro-American and the American Jew.*Westport, Connecticut: Negro Universities Press, 1970.

Witt, Shirley Hill, and Stan Steiner, eds. *The Way: An Anthology of American Indian Literature.* New York: Alfred A. Knopf, 1972.

Wright, Richard. *Black Boy: A Record of Childhood.* New York: Harper and Brothers, 1945.

–. *Native Son.* New York: Harper and Brothers, 1940.

—-. *Uncle Tom's Children.* New York: Harper and Brothers, 1940.

Index